A GAY MAN'S GUIDE TO LIFE

A GAY MAN'S GUIDE TO LIFE

GET REAL

STAND TALL

AND TAKE YOUR PLACE

BRITT EAST

HOUNDSTOOTH
PRESS

A GAY MAN'S GUIDE TO LIFE
Get Real, Stand Tall, and Take Your Place

ISBN   978-1-5445-0923-5 *Hardcover*
       978-1-5445-0922-8 *Paperback*
       978-1-5445-0921-1 *Ebook*
       978-1-5445-0924-2 *Audiobook*

CONTENTS

PREFACE

I wrote this book both for you and for me. It is for gay men, by a gay man, though certainly anyone is welcome to read it, and most of the concepts I present apply to us all. It is part personal growth and development manual, and part memoir. My lived experience is the source material; my story is the medicine. I want to transmute the pain of my past into the food of future growth, and to be the family I never had to gay men all over the world, so we might challenge and inspire each other to seize our lives and be our best selves.

I organized the chapters in this book to align with life's most important facets, and I make no bones about the fact that it represents life as seen through the lens of a gay man. I pull no punches and spare no one, but purposely save my toughest love for my own community. I want to challenge and inspire us, because I believe that in order to be empowered, we must own our truths, hold our journey, acknowledge our harms, atone, amend, and then move on.

You need not read this book sequentially, though you certainly could. I hope you will use my story and recommendations to prod you forward. I hope you will refer to topics of interest in this book whenever you need them as you move through life. I hope you will use this book as a guide to avoid the mistakes I made and claim some of the education you were perhaps denied, simply because of your sexual and cultural orientation.

But my greatest wish is that you ultimately use these words to lift others: your family, your friends, your coworkers, and your community—such that those who love us might know us a little better, those who follow us might have it a little easier, and those that hate us might learn to fear us a little less.

Real change requires sustained effort. It demands determination, self-discovery, personal practice, and relatedness. It insists on hustle and teamwork, takes energy and execution. And while there are no shortcuts, if you surround yourself with loved ones, hire experts, and work diligently, you will see results more quickly than you ever dreamed. This book will help you get real, and then get to work, so you can implement the practices you need to live your most audacious and authentic life, and truly start to thrive.

I know because this is what is working for me.

INTRODUCTION

MY STORY

In a gentler world, I might have lived in 1920s Paris or Berlin, spent my evenings with Brecht or Gertrude Stein, made love to Isherwood. But instead, I grew up in 1980s Tennessee—where intellectuals were punished, and differences destroyed. My world was an oblivion, and I stood naked and alone in the shadow of AIDS and the grip of homophobia.

In different times, my family could have been socialists who fought in the Spanish Civil War, or even marched in Montgomery—filling the house with poets and jazz, trading in dissent and manifesting vitality. But instead, they found suburban rage, and they set down their books, and they put away their music.

My friends might have been artists and intellectuals, members of the avant-garde, revolutionaries and anarchists. But instead, I had no friends and was no friend. And separateness became solitude, and daydreams became delusions, until all that might have been, never was.

I only ever longed to be loved because to be loved was to belong, and to belong was to be real. But our society is brutal, and our culture is primitive, so I spent my time living the lives of others. Meanwhile, the me of me that should have been was stuck back there—waiting to be born.

My family was like something out of Faulkner. We suffered without wisdom, steeped in denial and immersed in cycles of intergenerational trauma. Addiction. Abuse. Suicide. It's a myth that all parents love their children, just something we like to tell ourselves. A little lie that helps us keep things as they are, validates our own choices and inadequacies, and soothes our base instincts.

In my family, there wasn't a single way of hating ourselves, the world, or each other that we did not try—feasting on our own flesh, like wild animals that eat their young. They made it clear that everything about me was wrong: my body was a betrayal, my mind an extravagance, and my spirit a traitor. Society magnified what they had laid bare, and I knew that if I did not hide, I would be killed, ravaged by bigotry and homophobia. So I learned to fall through the cracks and slink in the shadows, to shed my dreams and relinquish my personality.

As a child, I would spend hours alone, dissociating while my mother and father raged. Their marriage was a crucible, and they rarely laughed or loved. Their parenting was steeped in cruelty, pushing me away when they should have been holding me close, writing my life's template, building my self-worth, and sowing the seeds of my future which I might one day carry forth to yield abundance, instead of the fallow field that was to come for so long.

Sure, they met some of their legal obligations. I was clean and clothed, relatively well-fed, sent to school. But that's about where it ended. They hollowed me out from the inside—draining me of all that was innately good, syphoning off any sweetness or stability that might sustain me, depriving me of family lineage and personal narrative. Most homosexual children don't get the chance to grow up in gay culture, but I grew up in no culture at all.

My family groomed me to serve their moods and relieve their stress. They needed to have someone they might control, a life they might squash, as theirs once was squashed. For them, I was nothing more than their outward reflection to the world. I did not exist in and of myself. What little they gave me was really just a gift to themselves, either to hurt each other or bolster their own self-image. They were focused more on their reputation than on anything real or meaningful. They had no bearing on what I wanted or needed. Instead, I endured their contradictory cycles of acclaim, abuse, and abandonment. So much was unspoken, unacknowledged, or outright denied. They traded in mutual delusion, and when I was eight years old, they divorced.

But they did not find freedom. Time only magnified their mutilations. They each spiraled down in their own ways, and I soaked up their bitterness, learned how to suffer, and milked my despondency. In school, I vacillated between invisibility and a desperate need for attention. I constructed a self-image based on middling performance and achievement, while inside I hid all that I lacked. But it never took long before I would inadvertently reveal myself through tears, gesture, or tone of speech.

I was just too tender-hearted for this world. And try as I might, I simply could not pass. In a misogynistic society, my femininity betrayed me. It wasn't just that I was homosexual—at that time there were no words for what I was: a beautiful blend of masculine and feminine traits that confounded most people I encountered. And that confusion often led to conflict, rejection, harassment, or even violence.

It was not long before I succumbed to despair and depression. I retreated into an entitlement rage that exacerbated my character defects and led me to dark places. I felt surrounded by boys, so many boys, and I was quaking with lust in this special hell. I longed for them to beat it out of me, this dangerous thing that had taken root, which made me inexcusably different. I weaponized my grief. I lied. I stole. I manipulated others. There was nothing I would not do in order to harm them or myself, just so long as we were all punished.

Believe me when I tell you that I was completely convinced of my own corruption. I was so sure of my brokenness that I longed to corrupt and break others. When your life is a lie, there is no truth, save the truth of mutual destruction. I hated weakness above all else, so I sharpened my fangs, desperately tried to grind down my sensitivities, disdained sympathy, and walked alone.

I painted my life in water, translucent and free, such that nobody would know me. I would seamlessly shift from class clown to defiant brat to feral animal—whatever it took to soothe this inchoate longing. I would pull people close, only to push them away. I had nothing and gave nothing to cling to. What might have been a cheeky, provocative nature, became purely oppositional and defiant, a way to reinforce my separateness, to stand alone for the sake of solitude—bolstering the feeling of my inevitable abandonment.

I lived in my own world, a reality based on delusion and dissociation. I scorned friendship and rejected those that would love me. It was not just the harm that I caused, but the opportunities I squandered, all that I might have learned, all that I should have practiced: friends I could have had, rites of passage missed, love lost. Nothing upon nothing, adding up to nothing. Just a tangled mess of toxic anxieties. My almost-life spread before me, always just out of reach, my personal history forever fading like a contrail.

By the time I left for college, my self simply had not formed. I was an empty shell, a husk. Less a full-fledged person than a collection of defense mechanisms, desperately seeking somewhere to hide, a refuge in the refuse. I didn't realize that so many of the other students would already know each other, and those that didn't had the tools to meet and make new friends, carve out a place for themselves, and wrestle the world. I had none of these skills.

It never occurred to me that with less structure and no foundation, relationships would be even more challenging in college than they were in high school. And without the familiar, warm blanket of my family's abuse and neglect, I was weightless. I did not fully land on campus. I floated as an apparition—drifting through classes and would-be social experiences, unable to form attachments, unjoined and unawake. I was only half there and oblivious to the danger that my freedom posed. Until one night, I swallowed fistfuls of pills, believing that everything God-like was gone. And that in the end, even when I lose, I win.

I remember it so clearly, that there was no one on the planet who knew where I was, cared how I was, if I was. It had been too easy to fall off the map, to drop out of time and space, to exist only in my thoughts. Nobody came to save me. And yet somehow, the next day, I woke up. I even went to class, ears ringing, head in a fog, but alive and trudging forward. I realized that the years of pain had brought me somewhere, that I was somehow purified. There was nothing left to burn. And I was ready to ask for help. I called a campus crisis line and was matched with my first therapist. I was determined to do something different.

Not long after, I met the first man I ever really loved. Oh, I had known boys, rough-housed on playgrounds, lurked in locker rooms, and lingered in showers. But this was a *man*, and our meeting was electric. He blew out my nervous system, forever changing me. It was now impossible for me to deny what I was, who I was. There was no escape, no going back.

Nothing had prepared me for the experience of being jolted from my body by another man. The cost of the closet is manifold, and I had no teachers. He was completely unavailable, yet tantalizingly close. And so instead of blossoming into romance, my lust devolved into obsession. I was a knot of codependency, and he kept reeling me in. He would tease me—luxuriating in my longing, only to shame me, use me, and then cast me aside. And I was happy to give him my power. Trapped in old patterns, I was desperate for someone to take care of me and hold me dear, in their highest good. But that requires integrity and selflessness, which each of us were lacking. He even outed me to our friends, perhaps to shift the spotlight from himself, or from us. Or maybe just out of cruelty.

For years it went on like this: my reaching for him, trying to win his attention, seducing him with levels of adoration that no one could match. I traded what little honor and dignity I had left, only for him to relent. Afterwards he would hate himself, and then hate me. I became more and more masochistic, dated other guys, and then ran back to him. The basis of tyranny is desire, and the insidious part of love is that it never leaves. It worms its way into everything you used to be. All you can do is watch and hold on.

In my own distorted way, I loved him. I was grateful that however broken I might have been, at least I was not yet completely dead inside. I had had an experience of what love was, or an inkling of what it might be. And yet even though it was obvious that this relationship was unhealthy for each of us, were it not for graduation, I might have forever lost myself. I saw it as my escape hatch, so after commencement, I left. I moved out of state, barely even said goodbye. Just like that, the leaves parted, and I found my way out.

I used graduate school as a life raft. Not only was it a wedge to pry me out of my prior circumstances, but it allowed me to use student loans to finance the next chapter. I arrived with my car filled with what little I owned, but no money, no housing, and no plan. All I had was an admission letter and a teaching assistantship. I would just have to figure the rest out on my own.

On the first day of class, I met a great guy and we fell in love. After all I had experienced, it was shocking that anybody would choose to love me. But love me he did. I still remember the moment we met, that tender mercy of finally finding someone like me. Previously my world had been so empty, and I could not dream larger than the next moment. For the first time, I experienced the joy of reciprocity: he wanted me as much as I wanted him. I no longer had to live with unrequited longing, the fear of being abandoned in a panic, or discarded out of disgust. But it had not yet occurred to me to cultivate my personal completeness prior to making a commitment, or that I was leaping into another relationship without first becoming whole—aborting what might have been a period of self-discovery. Instead, I was establishing the beginnings of a new pattern; it would leave me guessing at relatedness and fumbling through love for years to come.

In truth, I was awash in privilege: white, American, able-bodied, cisgendered, and ostensibly male. But with no real foundation, I was unable to leverage these privileges to build a sustainable, adult life. I careened from crisis to crisis, and mood to mood, no purpose and no ballast. In many ways, it was my relationship with my boyfriend that saved me. I threw all that I was into it, clung for dear life, hoped against hope that he might be my ticket to something better.

When we were apart, I thought I was nothing. And so I found myself sobbing on the phone one night, begging him to move in with me. Neither of us knew what we were doing.

But for some reason, he said yes. Back then, it was rather novel to have a steady boyfriend, especially at such a young age; living together was downright edgy. We knew of no one else who had even tried it.

We stayed there the better part of a year, and after my graduation moved to the big city. It was thrilling. I thought I had finally escaped the small town feeling that had haunted my childhood. Here was a place where I could be all of myself, wrapped in the cocoon of the gay ghetto. But although we were safe in the outside world, my inner world was still mush.

My boyfriend had to wear multiple hats. Not only was he my partner, but he was also my teacher and protector. I had handed him my entire life, which was patently unfair. He showed me how to get a job, how to save money, how to dream and set goals, how to have friends and be part of a family, what it was like to love God. And then he was arrested for having sex with a minor.

When the police came for him, they found me instead, alone in our apartment. There were two of them. They showed me their badges and forced their way in. They assumed I was him, and got aggressive, until I produced some ID. They told me why they were there, and what he had done. I was aghast, shaking my head in desperate confusion.

One of them pushed me, pinning me to the wall. I struggled to escape. He threatened me. Almost politely he asked me if I'd ever been hit, really been hit. If I knew what happens to people like us in prison. The other one trashed our apartment, looking for evidence. He said if I cooperated, they would leave. I just had to tell them where he was. I quickly relented and told them how to find him. They warned me not to call, said they would know if I alerted him. I was devastated, completely cracked open. Nothing had prepared me for this information, or the indignities of our criminal justice system. And even worse, it took so little for me to give in, to forsake the only man who had ever really loved me. With the mere threat of violence, I caved.

After they left, I called him. Certainly to warn him, but also to reclaim some shred of my dignity and show some solidarity. I have no idea what I said or how he responded. I have only flashes of what came next: he was arrested, found an attorney, and notified his parents. But what I remember most is a voicemail he left, while I was out doing God knows what. The sound of his voice was so broken and weak. He said that he was in lockup, and we had to hurry before they transferred him to jail for the weekend, where he would be incarcerated with the general population.

He told me what to do, how his parents were arranging bail. I just had to follow his instructions, and everything would be all right. The path was lain out for me. I remember thinking to myself that I don't have to do this. I could just run, take everything and disappear. Let him rot. But then I realized I had nowhere to go, that I was nothing without him. I had never built my own life. I replayed that voicemail over and over again, as proof that all of this was real. And to punish myself. Something about the smallness of his voice helped me savor the pain, feel the knife slide all the way in, one serration at a time.

I met with his attorney: fancy offices, leather everything,

pictures of this guy with members of Congress on the walls. I started to tell him the story, but he held up his hand. He said it wasn't necessary; he wasn't here for that. He was just going to make it all go away. And he was really good at that. It was his specialty. He already knew enough. This meeting was just about the money because nothing would happen without the money. How much money did we have, anyway? I told him, and he said fine, fine. That would be fine. This was all going to work out. This kind of thing happens all the time. He would take care of it. I emptied our savings to pay him. Lord knows none of it was my money anyway.

When my partner got home on bail, I was relieved but in denial. I guess I expected some sort of gratitude, that maybe he would love me even more, that this ordeal might actually strengthen our relationship, that we might be more committed than ever and could fight anything. I just assumed the worst was behind us. But instead, his disclosures kept coming. Once he started, he couldn't stop; his sense of relief was too profound. Turns out he was having lots of sex: countless partners on countless evenings, meeting guys online or in bathhouses, sneaking out while I was asleep. You name it, he had tried it. He didn't know if he could stop, made no promises, and was only marginally repentant.

Here was something else for which I was completely unprepared. I had no idea people did things like this, had never even heard of it before. We had shared a life for years. How would I ever begin to untangle our possessions, our finances, our friends, our home? I had never learned how to take care of myself, had no foundation from which to draw sustenance or wisdom, no real-life experience, and no family. I only knew how to run. So that's what I did.

I spent the summer travelling for work, focusing on building my music career. Afterwards, I returned for the hearing, which was all that you might imagine. My partner was white and came from money. This was his first offense. His fancy attorney knew the judge; they even talked about an upcoming golf trip. I remember lots of laughing. The young man was a person of color. It didn't take long for all charges to be dropped. You do the math. It was vile, and I felt awful about everything. I couldn't spend another second in his presence.

I took a job out of state, while my partner left the country to go find himself, trying to outrun his nightmare. Later that year he returned, and we were reunited. He admitted that his travels had not helped him conquer his demons. I felt miserable and was out of options. So we drifted back together, drawn by the gravity of love, shared history, and hopelessness. But part of the deal was that we had to move far away, leave that city and those memories behind. He wanted a fresh start and offered to bring me with him, like his little pet. And of course I was all too happy to hand over my power once again. I would have followed him anywhere, so we moved to the other side of the country.

Once we arrived, it was clear that nothing had changed. I was still holding us hostage, and he was still sneaking out. We each joined 12-step programs: he for sex addiction, and I for codependency. Of course I was apprehensive. Too focused on his faults, I was resistant to owning my part of the story. But slowly, and for the first time in my life, I got real. I found a sponsor, worked the steps, and lit my soul on fire. I had never witnessed such raw, unadulterated authenticity as in those meetings. It was electrifying. I admitted my powerlessness, created a fearless moral inventory, made amends, started service work, and bared my soul for the first time.

Even amidst this positive change, my partner and I split up, this time for good. We had shared more than six years together in our early twenties, which was no small feat for two gay men in the 1990s—a time when few in society acknowledged, much less celebrated, such relationships; a time when so many of our would-be role models had been cut down by the AIDS epidemic. There is so much we shared for which I am still grateful: laughter, adventure, and love. His fingerprints are all over my life, and we are friends to this day, as are our husbands.

But at the time, I was not able to let go of the harm. I was so naïve. On some level, I thought all my forgiveness had earned me something: the intimacy for which I had always longed, a kindness that might let my soul sleep. How was I to know that love incurs no debt, that slack senses offer no succor? So I left him, in a particularly ugly and passive-aggressive way, which was as much harm as I could muster.

After a few months of single life, I seized upon another relationship, signing up for more serial monogamy. But I was not yet a whole person, and was simply incapable of standing on my own. So of course I brought all my neediness, pain, and anguish to this relationship as well. I had learned some crucial life skills, and even cultivated some core values. But without a vision, mission, or purpose, I floundered. I just did not have enough sense of self to sustain my half of the equation, which was really too bad, because the love we shared was rich.

My new boyfriend opened a whole new world of intimacy and connectedness to me, and I was almost engulfed by the capacity of his spirit. I had never felt so seen as I did by him. It made me feel wanted and alive, joined in a way that I had never known. This alone healed many of my wounds and eased many of my anxieties. But it was also deeply threatening to be known so thoroughly. So I began to lull us to sleep and build a bunker. At a certain point, it became clear that I was hiding from the world in this relationship—holding him hostage, just like I had done with my previous partner. And after several years, he let me go.

It was also during this time that I severed all remaining ties with my family. They had ruined my life, aborted the life I might have had. My therapist at the time made it clear that this decision was mandatory if I truly wanted to reclaim my power and individuate as a full-fledged adult. I wrote letters to my parents, explaining everything. Letters that they could use as reference in the weeks ahead, when their minds might start to play tricks. Letters that spelled everything out in no uncertain terms, using words that should never have to be uttered.

I knew this choice would hurt them, but I focused on how they had hurt me. I allowed that anger to propel me forward. I held their funerals and mourned my losses. I made it clear to them that, while I found forgiveness fairly easy, I was incapable of forgetting. They would not rewrite my personal history. My story and dignity was not up for debate. I tempered any empathy with memories of that lost little boy, discarded by his family, savaged by the suburbs, and picked clean by society. So my reconciliation would never be with them, but with the truth of their behavior: what they chose to do to me every day and how they tried to erase my spirit. They abandoned me first.

It was clear that I needed some time flying solo. I had never truly taken care of myself. I had only ever been alone in the context of a romantic relationship: that insane dynamic of pulling my partner close, only to then hide from him. When I looked in the mirror, what I saw made me leave love after love, and made me love leaving. Because when we made love, my partners made me: whoever he was, I became. I had to remake myself into an image I might love, before allowing a partner to love me, or even make love to me.

I thought if I pared my life to the bone, I might master myself and gain some semblance of control. But that meant there was nobody on whom I could lean, and no one to do this dance with me. What made things worse is that I now had nowhere to turn. It is so tough moving through life without family. I had neglected to build a world of my own, did not know whose I was. I retreated further into myself and hunkered down. My objective was to seal myself from the world, such that nobody might ever see me or know me again. But instead of conjuring safety, I just ended up lonely and afraid. I learned that you can walk through this world as a wraith, haunting places in patterns of abject solitude, and nobody will necessarily stop you. Not one person is required to raise their head, look, and take notice.

I decided to take charge. I picked myself up and reentered society. I got a new job. I began volunteer work. Years went by. I met a wonderful man and we fell in love. Later we married and built a sweet life. But my baggage followed me. So I found a new therapist. Though he knew little of my world, he somehow had just the right energy to unlock my life. I have been seeing him for years, and he has created the single safest space I have ever known. He helped me unpack and contextualize my story, and challenged me to be kinder, gentler, more playful, and live with a lighter touch. He taught me that while I need to take care of business, I need not be the "CEO" of my life, that there is a grace that comes from letting life unfold of its own accord, and that the most effective progress is often made through indirect procedures. What I feel in that room is love, and that love has changed me. I got real, and then I got to work.

After years of telling my story, I still felt like something was missing. By this point, I was finally able to support myself financially. I had nearly two decades of experience in recovery and personal development work, had studied the 12 Steps, yoga, meditation, and nonviolent communication. And yet I knew there was more out there for me; I lacked a purpose and passion for life. So even though I knew I wanted to maintain my relationship with my therapist, I hired a life coach to complement that work and help me turn attitude into action.

My coach believes in me more than I have ever experienced. He helps me feel like I can take on the world and do just about anything. Where my therapist holds my story, my coach helps me manifest my dreams. He helps me shed my residual shame and internalized homophobia, while rewriting my personal narrative and stepping into my new life. Combined with the work of my therapist, my coach brought to light a whole new set of truths.

I've always been overly attuned to my own suffering. I spent years making love to my misery. I grew comfortable in the warmth of my sadness, soothed by my sorrow, safe in the arms of my self-fulfilling prophesies. I was dying to remain alone, which is pretty silly, since I only ever wanted to be cherished and adored, for others to see me and invest in what they saw, and to experience the thrill of togetherness.

I'm often overly idealistic, and struggle to live life on life's terms. I immerse myself in fantasy, so I might preserve my illusions of control, paper over my pain, and hide from the endless parade of my past absurdities. I place impossible expectations on those that would love me. These resentments reinforce my core belief that I am permanently broken and alone. But I must be a friend before I can have a friend. That means mining my depths and transmuting my trauma today, so that tomorrow I might love you.

I am not unique, and neither of us are alone. If you want to change your life, you must get real and then get to work. You've got to get real about who you are and the life you've led. Get real about your choices, your fear, and your anger. Get real about your family and your childhood programming. Get real about your body, your mind, and your spirit. This is a matter of rigorous honesty, about looking at your life and accurately measuring its hills and valleys.

You cannot do this alone. You must meet yourself in the eyes of others: those who can reflect your character defects while celebrating your emerging self. You also need someone to help give you context and proportion to your story, so you can examine your motives, the results, the unintended consequences, and above all, so you can be joined in them. This can be a mental health professional, a coach, a mentor, a group, a congregation, whatever. Be relentlessly pragmatic. Do what works.

After you get real, it is your personal practice that will sustain your progress. I made a sacred commitment regarding the primacy of my own health, the essentiality of my own wellness, and the urgency of my own self-care, such that I might once again be whole, have something to give, and be able to show up to my life with light and love. This is a daily set of activities that moves me to a heart space and connects me both to my inner child and divine guidance.

The core of my practice is based on movement and embodiment, because nothing spiritual is truly separate from the body. You must find a way to fall in love with your physical form. You are beautiful and desirable just as you are, so start acting like it. This is less about feeling pretty than about feeling grateful. This part of my practice involves a combination of yoga, walking, and weightlifting. So get moving. Literally. Stand tall and take up space. Be seen and be heard as you transform into your confident, radiant self. Walk with dignity and pride. Act like the warrior that you are meant to be, then take your place in this world.

Stepping into this new life is one thing, but bonding with your better self is another. Spend time dreaming. Meditate. Create the space necessary to learn both what you believe and what you need. Go on adventures. Cultivate the hobbies and passions that will sustain you. The bottom line is that you need to get to know this new person, who is more you than you have ever been. What do you envision? What do you value? What and whom do you love?

I believe that we are all in this together; that if each of us took a little less, we would all have a whole lot more; and that there is no greater wisdom than kindness. I have never known a love like this, this love that I learned to feel for myself and each of you, that lights me on fire and sets me free. It's as if I have been cracked open by the blessing of just walking with you, and the me of me that was always meant to be is at long last being born.

CHAPTER 1

BODY

The very first thing I remember hating was my body. It was my body that betrayed me, that longed for physical contact with other boys and prevented my entrance into the idealized masculine. It wasn't my fault: it was my body's feminine voice, swishy gestures, and secret desires. Homosexuality was dangerous, and it was my body that was under siege. That's why I couldn't stand the sight or sound of my body, didn't dare look at myself in the mirror or in photos. Audio and video recordings were disastrous. They forced me to confront what the world met when it met me: a sissy. Which is to say that I was tender-hearted and gender-nonconforming, not meant for the world of straight men.

When I was growing up, popular culture only magnified this message. Newscasts reduced our lives to gruesome images, withering under the weight of AIDS. Movies washed us away altogether, leaving us as little more than innuendo. In sitcoms, we only existed as stereotypes, adding sassy color to the lives of the main characters. And by main characters, of course I mean the real men with real bodies, who represented real people.

Society magnified my solitude by saturating me with shame—reflecting all that I would never be. Straight people called me repulsive, threatened me with bodily harm, and ensured I would have no sense of self or well-being. My body was unsafe and unwelcome. When I came out to my mother, it was my body she attacked, spitting words of disease and disgust. Erasing my body was tantamount to erasing my story, a story she simply could not afford. So I grew up with no place and no culture, no tribe and no initiations. All because of my body.

I had no form or function, so I dissociated. Lost in thought, I lived like a ghost. At its heart, this was an abnegation of my body. I attempted to detach from the root cause of this harm, to cut out the cancer, which just happened to be all of me. I tried to cobble together a facade that might pass, be less threatening to the world's fragile masculinity. I played sports. I wore the right clothes. I tried to say the things that boys should say. But it was my body that would always bring me back, inadvertently revealing my undesirable aspect, combined with a desperate and driving desire: to both be them and have them.

I ritualized my fantasies, as if I might gain some control. I would constrain and distort my lust until it was unrecognizable, a faint echo of normalcy. But my body was patient and cunning. It led me to idealized friendships bound by unspoken truths. It lured me to the intoxicating combination of lust and fear, followed by the inevitable look of disgust and disdain. I hated them, and I hated myself. That cycle went on until the arc of my life that should have bent toward togetherness instead broke toward isolation. And then I cast my body aside, without even a second glance.

It was my body that rose and hobbled forth, forcing me to continue, insisting I go on. I spent years like this: falling and rising like some fey Frankenstein. I wasted so much time, not realizing that the very parts of me I hated were precisely what some people desired. Completely unaware of my privilege, I was mired in self-pity. It wasn't until I finally learned that my body is the basis of my humanness that I began to love myself.

No matter who you are, what you do, or where you've been, you are having a human experience. Everything you do, or say, or think, or feel, is grounded in your humanness. And there is nothing more human about you than your body. This is true regardless of your race or ethnicity. It has nothing to do with your age or weight. From professional athletes to office workers, the able-bodied to those living with physical limitations or disabilities. It does not matter how much money you have, or how popular you are. Regardless of your sexual orientation, your gender identity or expression, or your cultural identity, this principle remains the same: the experience of our bodies unites us all.

Even if you believe you are more than your body, it is your body that anchors your experience. Right where you are, right now. Spirituality starts with the body, and there is no enlightenment without embodiment. You might experience the purest thoughts and feelings of kindness, but until that kindness is expressed through your body, it will come to precious little. It will remain trapped in your mind and in your spirit, inaccessible to the outside world. If you truly want to be of service, at some point you must convert your thoughts and feelings into work. When we put attitude into action, an alchemy that transmutes wishes into reality, we convert dreams to deeds. This is the magic of incarnation, spirit made manifest through the body, such that it might yield tangible results. That's why when we do good, we say we "touch someone's life," as in physically, with our hands.

GETTING REAL ABOUT BUILDING YOUR TEAM

If you are out of integrity with your body, it is your humanness that is at risk: that part of you destined to do, go forth, experience, give, love, and live. Nutrition and physical fitness are moral imperatives. If your body is the intercessor between your loving thoughts and actions, then nourishing your body is the first step to nourishing your soul and serving humanity.

You can only give what you have, so if you want to serve the world, you must serve yourself first. It all starts with intention. Once you acknowledge where you are, you can identify where you want to go and stake your claim on how to get there. What do you want your body to feel like? Where do you want your body to take you? How can your body be of service to others? Getting clear on these intentions is crucial because you will need to communicate them to your team: those friends, family members, and experts who will support you, hold you accountable, and help make your dreams a reality.

Here is a list of key team members you will need by your side on this journey:

- Family
- Friends
- Primary care physician
- Secondary healthcare practitioners
- Personal trainer (optional)
- Yoga instructor, or equivalent (optional)

Sustenance is that combination of healthy food and exercise we need to "sustain" our bodies through practice. This routine is best built slowly, one brick at a time, with the counsel of experts and loved ones. The first team member you should consult is a medical professional: someone you will entrust to monitor your health, ensure that your goals match what your body can realistically achieve, and that your strategies and tactics will not derail any other facet of your life.

Establish a relationship with a primary care physician, then schedule an appointment for a routine physical, where you can share your initial intentions. If you have not recently engaged in a regular practice of physical fitness, it's important to get this outside perspective. While I'm a fan of alternative (naturopathic) medicines, I think Western (allopathic) medicine does a great job treating acute injuries and illnesses. You will want this relationship in place and well established, in case of any physical fitness-related injuries or issues down the line. My advice is to use both modalities: allopathic medicine for the precise treatment of acute conditions, and naturopathic medicine for the holistic treatment of chronic conditions.

GETTING REAL ABOUT YOUR FOOD

The easiest change most of us can make is to improve the

quality of the foods we put into our bodies. I encourage you to spend some time counting the calories you eat and drink each day, as well as the associated mix of macronutrients (protein, carbohydrates, fats, etc.). This practice is about self-awareness, not fashion or culturally contrived beauty myths. When I started counting calories, I was shocked at how much I was inadvertently eating and drinking. My lack of awareness had resulted in my ingestion of too many calories, as well as an unhealthy ratio of macronutrients. I bought a simple bathroom scale and found a program to help me determine my Total Daily Energy Expenditure (TDEE): a calculation of caloric intake versus output. I then synchronized everything to the pedometer on my smartphone to track my exercise.

By monitoring the foods and beverages I consumed, I was able to take charge of my nutrition, without dieting or deprivation. It also had the added benefit of forcing me to get educated about the ingredients in everything I was eating and drinking. That helped me home in on exactly what needed to change. Adjusting a few key areas made a huge difference. Recent advances in technology have made it much simpler to scan the barcodes of groceries and prepared foods. It is easier than ever to monitor your nutrition and maintain an optimal caloric intake and ratio of macronutrients.

Let's face it: food is political. For much of American history our racist, classist, and homophobic laws and policies have prevented many of us have from having consistent access to nutritious food in our neighborhoods. In some cases, we lacked the capacity to prepare healthy meals, fell through the cracks, and were forced to rely on pre-packaged foods without the requisite nutrition to sustain us. In other cases, our very lives were illegal and our bodies were under assault. Some of us were purged from our families and forced to flee our towns in the name of survival. We left our land and our fields for urban centers—harboring dreams of a life with those like us, minimizing as much bigotry as we could.

Some of us had trouble sustaining consistent and gainful employment. We were barred from access to polite society, turned to addictive substances and behaviors to fill the void, and were forced into a climate ripe for organized crime and police misconduct. Our neighborhoods became ghettos, and those businesses that might have offered support, stayed away. So it should come as no surprise that it is often tough for some of us to find fresh produce, much less a gym, a yoga class, or any other healthy alternative based on our abilities. And when we finally do find these things, we often can't afford them. We resort to unhealthy convenience out of weariness, poverty, or fatigue, and continue our downward intergenerational spiral.

Food is also cultural, and many of us were not taught how to prepare nutritious meals. Over the course of time, our persistent disenfranchisement changed our personal landscapes. It altered our behaviors and opportunities, and eventually led to new cultural norms. In the case of food, our lack of access to healthy ingredients became codified in our family recipes: a story of deprivation handed down from one generation to the next as we made do with what we had.

I grew up in the southern US, where much of our food was unhealthy. What might have started as a technique to disguise its lack of freshness, over time, fried and overcooked food became the norm. In some places, our ingredients were often the old and unused scraps of plants and animals that respectable society would not buy, and which might otherwise become garbage. While we learned how to make the best of these situations, we were still operating from profound disadvantages. Yes, we were able to turn offal and scraps into delicious dinners in order to feed our family, but often at the expense of nutrition.

Some of us grew up in suburban blight, born into lives of mass media and hyper-consumption, and surrounded by excess. We normalized pre-packaged food and became paralyzed by an abundance of choice. Our decision-fatigue led to apathy. We lost our curiosity and stopped talking to farmers, produce workers, and butchers. We set aside our family recipes and heritage. We stopped reading labels and fell under the spell of marketing. We lost our connection to the land and the tradition of family meals. We often ate in front of our televisions, at our desks, or in our cars.

That this food was loaded with salt and preservatives did our bodies no favors. We traded balance for convenience. We forgot about fruits and vegetables altogether. We stopped drinking water in favor of sodas and coffees filled with high fructose corn syrup, opting for frequent hits of sugar and caffeine to get us through the next few minutes of the day. This quick fix was an attempt to bolster us and change our mood, to drown our pain and help us manufacture the feeling of being alive. These beverages not only dehydrated us, but also added empty calories to our diets.

GETTING REAL ABOUT YOUR ADDICTIONS

Many of us have used food for reasons other than nourishment. We ate in order to sublimate our feelings, or out of addiction. Addiction is any unmanageable, compulsive, mood-altering behavior, and can certainly include eating. This combination can be devastating to our physical fitness. While it's healthy to recognize our past, and empowering to acknowledge the reality of our situation, it serves none of us to dwell in it. It's neither impossible nor too late for us to take charge of our lives. We may have grown up in unhealthy situations or with bad habits, but we can change. I'm living proof of that.

I used to self-soothe with food. I often ate beyond what it took to feel full and used food to manage my stress, anxiety, and loneliness. What I ate was steeped in the comfort food of the southern US: high in saturated fats and carbohydrates, fried everything, overcooked vegetables, and way too many sodas. It's taken me years to change my palate and learn how to gauge a true feeling of fullness. But I've finally reached a place where I refrain from overeating and happily avoid excess salt and sugar. If you think you might be suffering from compulsive eating or an addiction to food, there are many resources available to you. You don't have to suffer in silence or do this alone.

Of course, food and beverages are not the only substances many of us have used in the name of addiction. Aside from the various natural substances we have turned to (such as alcohol, tobacco, marijuana, etc.), we have sublimated our pain through the use of various synthetic drugs as well. I think the average person would be horrified to learn the various ingredients found in drugs like meth or ecstasy.

Even controlled substances, like cigarettes, with naturally occurring key ingredients, contain many toxic, synthetic additives. While we might not consider this at the time that we choose to ingest these substances, I think deep down most of us realize their danger. Part of the thrill is their deleterious effects on our bodies, if not also their illegality.

There are all sorts of reasons we self-harm. However, it behooves us to get clear on the consequences of both the short-term and long-term impacts on our bodies, as well as the possible unintended consequences and associated opportunity costs. In some cases, through no fault of our own, our life experience or mental health might adversely impact our ability to make healthy choices. In those situations, we might need to ask for help and rely on professionals or loved ones for assistance. The rest of us should take regular, rigorous looks at everything we put in our bodies. I advise you to spend a week listing every substance you ingest, including food, alcohol, tobacco, drugs, etc. That list is your baseline. Next to each item, include an associated intention: do you plan to continue using or ingesting this substance at current levels, or do you intend to alter or even end your consumption? If so, for how long? Be specific. We must all begin at the beginning; there is no shame in starting where you are.

If you have any physical, mental, or emotional challenges that make meal prep a struggle, you might consider creative alternatives, such as purchasing pre-cut vegetables for healthy snacking. If there are periods during which your symptoms lessen, you might utilize them to focus on procuring and preparing food, so it's ready to go for the rest of the week. The key is that we marshal what resources we have, so we can get empowered and then get to work on taking care of our bodies. We all start this journey from different places and have different goals, but for each of us, physical health and wellness is at the root of our well-being.

For me, the tipping point of finally choosing to take care of my body was chronic insomnia. Consistent sleep loss had gotten painful enough to incentivize me to take stock of my life and change my behaviors. It became clear that I was consuming too much alcohol and caffeine. My body never liked this stuff anyway. But over the years, it had become a social and emotional crutch. I decided to experiment with how my sleep might improve without these substances, so I dramatically cut my alcohol and caffeine consumption. Sure, there were some social consequences, not to mention a few rough weeks of withdrawal symptoms as my body cleansed and detoxed. But afterwards, I quickly realized I didn't miss these things at all. And my friends and family got over it. Most importantly, I immediately started to notice a positive impact on my sleep patterns.

As I found my way back to better physical fitness, I started more closely monitoring the food I ate. I made a list of the healthy snacks that I would allow myself to consume each day. That way there was never a question: if it wasn't on the list, I didn't eat it. After I normalized that change, I added desired quantities of each food per snack. I tend to keep myself really busy and don't have time to think through things deeply during the day. But I knew that if it was on my list, I would be able to stick to it. This list was an invaluable tool for me. In fact, I had so much success getting my snacking under control that I expanded my list to include breakfasts and lunches. I found a way to focus on easy-to-prepare meals, consisting mainly of protein and healthy carbohydrates.

In our house, my husband cooks dinner, so I saved that meal for last. I had demonstrated months of healthy eating, without ever really discussing it with him. So, by the time I brought it up, the conversation was easy; he was all too happy to adjust. After avoiding a healthy eating practice for years, it was actually surprisingly simple to implement. What I had once feared as deprivation, now actually felt like abundance, because I had shifted my thinking. At no part of this process did I feel like I was on a "diet."

GETTING REAL ABOUT YOUR CARDIOVASCULAR EXERCISE

As I improved my eating habits, I also started spending more time outside. I am a homebody by nature, and most days I resemble a housecat. But as much as I hate to admit it, our bodies belong outside. Indoors is the realm of the mind, but outdoors is the realm of the body—where we might move, stimulate our senses, and get our blood flowing; where we can warm our skin in the sun, feel the wind in our hair, and connect with nature. We were not born to live inside office buildings or sit in chairs for extended periods of time. Our bodies are meant to be in motion.

I encourage you to spend as much time outdoors as possible. Few of us have any excuses. Almost all of us have the ability to walk around the block, or at least to the mailbox. Most of us can park a little farther away from the door, just to get in a few extra steps. When the weather truly makes it unwise to be outside, almost all of us can spend ten minutes walking on a treadmill or at the mall. Once we get a clean bill of health from our healthcare professional, it's up to us to honor our intentions and get moving, to fight for our own health and wellness. Start small and increase the time, speed, and distance a little each week. Soon you will feel the full benefits of endorphins, stress reduction, and energy increase. And before you know it, you will even start looking forward to this part of your day, until what was once only life-enhancing has become essential.

Depending on your previous average activity levels, you might encounter new forms of physical stress. That's perfectly natural. The key is to learn the difference between healthy and harmful pain. It takes time and experience to build this intuition, but there are some general hallmarks of harmful pain. When in doubt, watch your breath. If you find yourself holding your breath, then something is probably wrong. Breathing is an involuntary bodily function; any holding of the breath is some sort of message. If you notice that you are holding your breath, stop what you're doing, and return to the present moment. Shift your attention to your intention. Let go. Unless something is seriously wrong, your breath will quickly return, and then you can resume your activity.

A subtler indication of harmful pain is the difference in sensation between the pain of contraction (such as muscle cramping) and the pain of expansion (such as healthy muscle stretching). In general, a sharp pain of contraction is a warning, while the slower pain of expansion is the result of growth. Again, stop what you're doing and find your breath. Mentally scan your body. Monitor the sensations. Slowly resume the exercise as you feel ready, while paying special attention to the location of your previous pain. Experiment to find a pain-free range of motion for whatever movement you're doing. If you would like to learn more about this, there is a lot of great literature out there on the topic, and of course, I highly encourage you to dialog with your health-care professionals and physical fitness team.

I am fortunate to have been introduced to team sports at an early age. Youth soccer was popular in my suburban neighborhood, and my parents placed me on a team when I was five years old. Although their motives were somewhat suspect (apparently they were worried I was too "feminine"), it was a decision that changed the arc of my life. Not only did I normalize the pain of physical fitness and the thrill of competition, I developed a passion for the sport, and athletics in general. At a time when so many gay boys were afraid of the bullying and harassment that seemed inevitable in these situations, I flourished, simply because I was good at the game. It became an entry into a world of boys I might otherwise not have had. Of course it also brought up a whole host of other issues, since I was completely lacking in any loving foundation or support. But in general, I feel grateful for the experience.

As an adult, I was able to leverage that hobby in all sorts of social situations. I even played for some intramural teams in a gay soccer club. The point is this: I am privileged to have been given this opportunity at such a young age. Even though I was unprepared to reap all of its rewards, I savored all that I could. Somehow, I didn't give it up. I used my past rewards as a springboard to build a future that would sustain me. I recognize that not everyone has positive associations around sports and athletics, and that's okay. There are all sorts of strategies to help rewrite those stories. From gay sports leagues to workout buddies, it's important to realize that you don't have to do this alone. You are not at the mercy of your past. You can take the good parts and use them as sustenance for the life you want to create.

GETTING REAL ABOUT YOUR RESISTANCE TRAINING

Once you normalize a regular routine of cardiovascular movement, I encourage you to add some form of resistance training to your practice. Personally, I love weightlifting, but your practice might take other forms. Check with your healthcare professional before implementing this next phase, then join a gym with a broad array of workout equipment. That way you can share facility and equipment costs with other members, rather than buying everything yourself. If you have the resources, you might also hire a personal trainer. Many gyms offer free initial assessments with potential personal trainers. If you try to go it alone, just be aware that it is easy at this stage to let your excitement get the best of you and quickly injure your body. Always take precautions when weight training, whether on your own or with friends.

A personal trainer will work with you one-on-one to help get you started on the right foot. Their role is to build a predictable, repeatable process with you, collaboratively, which you can then carry forth on your own. They will help you start slowly with the type and level of resistance training that is right for you. They will work with you to find pain-free ranges of motion on key muscle groups. If you don't have the extra money for a personal trainer, there are tons of great articles, blog posts, podcasts, and videos on any number of platforms. At the end of the day, you are your own best advocate, and nobody knows your body better than you. It is up to you to absorb all the information you can and then synthesize it—building the practice that is right for you.

In resistance training, it's important to work the body to a level of discomfort, without putting yourself at risk. Muscle fibers must be slightly torn during workouts, so they can grow larger and stronger during recovery periods. It is important you learn to feel the differences in sensations between this normal and healthy process, as opposed to an injurious muscle pull or strain. Again, it will take time and experience to build your intuition. Recurring consultations with your healthcare professionals and personal trainer will ensure you stay on the right track.

I tend to give about 75–85 percent of my total effort in any single resistance training exercise. The last thing I want to do is injure myself. I work out alone, and so have no one to spot me or help me out of a jam; so perhaps I'm overly cautious. This effort level is just a subjective and arbitrary numeric range, but implies I still have some gas in the tank after each set. I'm focused on building a sustainable practice of health and wellness, and not trying to win any awards. That intention gives me the freedom to go slowly and to put in the workout reps mindfully. It allows me to honor my body, listen to my fears, and respect my boundaries.

If you stay present during your workout, I suspect you will notice that you feel and think all sorts of things. Merely blowing past these thoughts and feelings can be a form of self-harm. Instead, honor the thoughts in your mind and the sensations in your body. Observe the thoughts in your mind. Cultivate a sense of humor and nonattachment to the results. Get curious. This attitude will help you avoid injury and stay on the right path. Just be honest with yourself. If you're having a bad day and need to leave the gym early, or skip your workout altogether, that's fine. In your heart of hearts, you will know if you're avoiding something or just honoring your sweet soul. Take care of yourself, but don't kid or coddle yourself. There might be reasons for your choices, but there are no excuses.

When I first started weightlifting, I was fortunate that my boyfriend at the time was also passionate about it. He happily shouldered the research burden, and I just followed along. It was like he was my own personal trainer. I recognize how tough it might have been, had I been forced to do all that research myself. There is so much information out there; it can be really intimidating. That's why I believe in working with experts. In most cases we have to hire them, but sometimes we're lucky enough to have a friend or loved one on whom we can lean. We can ask them for help, or at least to point us in the right direction. Even if they don't have the time to take us under their wing, most people are happy to share what worked for them and then put us in contact with a trained professional.

While hiring experts can be a financial burden, I look at it as a way to pay ourselves first. What better investment can there be than the health and wellness of our bodies? What could possibly yield better returns? I prefer to pay a personal trainer now than a surgeon somewhere down the line. Either we invest in our health today, or we will have to invest in the treatment of our illnesses or injuries tomorrow. If you're worried about finances, think of it like this: how much are your Band-Aids and stress-management crutches costing you? If you simply shift some of those resources to invest in your physical fitness, you might actually save money in the long run, without noticing much immediate deprivation. There is an entire spectrum of costs and cost-savings for a wide variety of income and commitment levels. In this day and age, there is help out there for almost all of us.

Many Band-Aids are actually helpful, or even necessary. Just about all of us require some bolstering each day, due to our circumstances. The key is to be honest with yourself about any associated costs. Is your Band-Aid distracting you from an underlying issue or root cause? For instance, if your neurological makeup means you require specific stimuli to stay focused, there is likely nothing detrimental about it. But if you choose to self-medicate, you will likely do well to consult with a trained healthcare provider in order to craft more effective solutions and minimize any associated risks. Some stress management tools last a lifetime, and that's okay. Just be clear about your choices.

GETTING REAL ABOUT YOUR STRETCHING

As you increase your cardiovascular activity and start to build and tone muscle, you will notice your body feeling unnaturally tight. I like to use yoga as my third pillar of physical fitness, but implementing any form of regular stretching and core strengthening will help. If you decide to go the route of yoga or Pilates, I encourage you to attend classes in person. One-on-one sessions are typically unnecessary for beginners. While books and videos are certainly helpful, regular face-to-face contact with a qualified professional will allow you to build a relationship. They will get to know your body over time. In many cases, they will work with you to help you train your body. Even stretching and core strengthening can induce injury, so it's critical to take care of yourself.

It's also important to socialize with others that carry similar intentions. Personal connections will help you form positive experiences and break bad habits. In class settings, you will meet others with similar challenges, issues, and struggles. You will find a place to be joined in your successes and celebrate your wins. Plus, it's fun! Yoga studios frequently have the added benefit of offering associated services in addition to their traditional asana classes. Studying breath work, attending meditation classes, learning about yogic theories and philosophies, and participating in devotional singing all can help you build community while you nurture your body.

It was in yoga classes that I first learned to distinguish the sensations in my body. I realized just how disconnected I had become, how much I was carrying around with me, and how much there was to heal. Through studying the yoga sutras (theory and philosophy), singing kirtan (devotional chants), and practicing both pranayama (breath work) and the asanas (postures), I developed my first body-mind-spirit connection. Those early days were so blissful and fun, as this new world opened up to me. It was love at first seated twist! When my partner at the time returned from a lengthy trip to India, he signed up for a few classes in a local studio. I made relentless fun of him at first, but over time I watched this man who had trouble committing to a slice of toast, commit to these classes. It was beautiful, and I was filled with envy. So I decided to tag along!

I knew I would have trouble sticking to this routine without some financial commitment. I needed some skin in the game. So together we invested in an early morning yoga immersion series. We pre-paid for several classes a week over the course of a month, and had a blast. Afterwards, we would even have breakfast together at a local cafe, before starting the workday. But as that first immersion series concluded, he decided that he was done. The classes were just too early for him. But me on the other hand...well, let's just say I was in love with this new world. I continued with that series for an entire year.

When we moved to a different neighborhood, I simply changed yoga studios. And it was in this new studio that I found a home. Their flavor of yoga just resonated with every part of me. I even did a teacher training with that studio, in order to further my studies. This was in the relatively "early" days of modern American yoga; there were never very many guys in a given class. But there were several guys in that teacher training, and it felt like we were charting some new ground, opening doors for others.

There are so many forms of physical activity out there just waiting for you. Find one that is fun, that lifts your spirit, that you look forward to. Do that, and you can build an emotional connection that will drive your discipline.

GETTING REAL ABOUT FALLING IN LOVE WITH YOUR BODY

Over the course of your fitness journey, you will invariably encounter illnesses, distractions, and lapses in motivation. That's okay. It's all part of the process. During these times, focus on your original intention: making slow and steady incremental progress, in order to build a sustainable practice based on health and wellness. I can't tell you how many times I've had to step away from parts of my physical fitness practice, either due to illness, injury, time constraints, or for any other number of reasons. But because I try to keep a beginner's mind, I am never too distraught. Sure I might feel annoyed or disappointed, but because I have tried and failed so many things so many times in life, I am well-acquainted with the process and pleasure of beginning again: picking myself up, dusting myself off, chuckling at the situation, and then getting back to it. If you're in it for the long haul, who cares about missing a week? Or even a month? There are no shortcuts. But who wants them anyway? The journey truly is both the goal and the reward.

Along the way you will inevitably encounter experts who are full of beans or simply don't gel with your personality. When this happens, you can either look past these differences and persist, or source a new expert. There's no sense in abandoning your intentions just because you come across one instructor that you happen to dislike. Either ride it out and get curious (Ask yourself what's beneath your discomfort? What's behind your aversions to their personality? Etc.), or just move along to the next expert! The main thing is to persist in your commitment.

After more than two decades of working on my own personal growth and development, I know this for certain: you must find some way to fall in love with your body. Even if only just a part of it, even if only just for today. You cannot heal what you do not love. When it comes to loving your body, sometimes all you need is exposure therapy (there's a pun in there somewhere). I started by spending most of my time at home completely naked. I was having so much trouble getting comfortable in my own skin, and I figured that if I didn't get used to seeing my own nakedness, I would never set down my shame. Believe me, as someone who spent years hating my body, I know just how this sounds. But I'm telling you, it really helped!

Over time, my mind started to wander, and I forgot how horrible I thought I looked while washing the dishes in the nude, or running the vacuum with my moobs jiggling. And as even more time passed, I stopped cringing whenever I caught a glimpse of myself in the mirror. Finally I actually looked forward to those moments alone, when I could make it home and strip off all my clothes, to dust the shelves in the buff. As long as you're not trapped in some beauty myth, there's nothing wrong with wanting to look good naked, whatever looking "good" means to you. The point of self-empowerment is that you get to decide. To a certain degree, you get to choose what your body looks like. And the rest, you get to let go of, laugh at, and giggle about with your friends, who are all struggling with this issue, just like you.

If you do not create an emotional connection with your body, you will not change. If you do not learn to see yourself in a whole new way, there will be no reason to shed your past behaviors. Most habits are just too tough to break without the care and concern of others: the comradery of loved ones, joining us in our intentions, helping hold our accountability and celebrating our successes. But attitude and connection alone are not enough to sustain us. It's our daily choices and actions that build motivation and momentum. Elevating your awareness and attunement of this interplay allows you to shed culturally constituted concepts like fatness and thinness, and move beyond physical appearances. In doing so, you can reject the beauty myth, step into a new way of being, and embrace the embodiment of your values, such that you might love yourself and change the world. With your body.

SUMMARY

There is no health and wellness without a healthy body. Your relationship with your body is at the heart of every experience you have. Most of us need to hire a team of experts to support our physical fitness journey. You cannot do this alone, nor should you have to. Your relationship with food reflects your relationship with your body. There is no health without nutritious food and beverages. Food is both political and cultural, but we must break free of our intergenerational trauma if we are to build the life of our dreams. In some cases, we have sought refuge in food. Over time, that behavior can turn compulsive, and sometimes into a full-fledged addiction.

Addiction is any unmanageable, compulsive, mood-altering behavior. It is rampant in all communities, including gay men. If you think you might be struggling with an addiction, there are any number of resources available to you. But at the end of the day, you must take a rigorous look at your life in order to change your behavior. Any well-rounded program of physical fitness needs to utilize three components:

- Cardiovascular exercise
- Resistance training
- Stretching

The only way to beat motivation loss and stay engaged in your physical fitness journey is to make an emotional connection with your goals. Habits are just too tough to break otherwise. The most effective way to do this is to fall in love with your body. It might sound corny, but if you can learn to love this part of you, given enough time, energy, and support, the rest of your program will start to fall into place.

CHAPTER 2

MIND

There was a time, not so long ago, when I thought I might be consumed by my mind—the part of me that longed to fade from this world, disapparate. It was my mind that told me I was worthless, that I deserved to be abandoned and alone. It was my mind that swore I was helpless and hopeless. That I must cling to others for survival, that I could not manage my life on my own.

These thoughts did not come out of thin air. My family instilled them in me, society reinforced them, and my mind embraced them. I was surrounded, immersed. I internalized everything, until any dissonance between my personal experience and the messages I received from the world eroded away. I absorbed all of it, until all that was left of me was an array of false beliefs, fear-based perceptions, and missed opportunities. I was reduced to a broken spirit. I mingled stories of deprivation and scarcity with denial, that I might never know the light of love or the call of being claimed, and my world might melt into nothingness.

During those times when I attempted to engage with others, I had no supporting foundation or framework. I never learned how to relate to anyone in a healthy way. That meant I was simultaneously writing the template of my life and living it. This involved lots of guesswork, trial, and error. In social situations, my brain received stimuli of fear and anxiety. This drove my mind to grasp for control, to overengineer interpersonal relationships, and to create predetermined outcomes. I tended to rationalize and over-intellectualize everything, which might have worked, but for my equally desperate need to be seen and known.

My mind created a personality of fear and self-loathing, an identity written in water, based on nothing. I was caught in the middle of two competing extremes: the irresistible force of validation (interdependence) and the immovable object of fear (my mind). It's no wonder I became paralyzed and confused. Naturally, it was my mind that won. It locked me away and hid me for years in a misguided attempt to keep me safe. But the universe has a way of forcing us out of our cages, whether we are ready or not. I was not. With no wisdom or experience, I lacked perspective and propor-tionality. I replayed every interpersonal interaction with a sense of dysphoric recall and recrimination—cringing at each moment in which I inadvertently revealed myself. What I did not realize is that the magic of interrelatedness lies in mutual vulnerability. It requires letting go, holding hands, and jumping in.

GETTING REAL ABOUT YOUR ATTITUDE

Thriving in modern society means learning how to effectively harness and channel our outrage. We must acknowledge the many brutal truths of the world, so that we can work to change them. But we must also temper those truths with the reality of our abilities and capacities. Each of us has finite time on this planet, as well as significant constraints on what we can learn and accomplish. None of us can do it all, and especially not alone. If we truly want to get somewhere, we must go together.

The richness of life comes when we embrace our limits. As soon as we acknowledge the fact that there is only so much each of us can do to improve our world, then we are free to release all that we cannot do. We can create space for others to shine, as well as room for our own joy; this is essential to building anything sustainable. When we first start to experience empowerment, it can be so tempting to go overboard, to think we can be everywhere and fix everything. We act as if all we must do is think the right combination of thoughts, or say the right combination of words, and the universe will suddenly open up to us, like some cosmic cash machine. But the destination is the journey. There are no finish lines, and there will never be a time when the world is perfectly at rest.

There are many personal growth and development teachers who wrap themselves in blankets of delusion. Some are charlatans, basking in their own wealth and privilege. Others are simply inexperienced and misguided, insisting you can have whatever you want, as long as you ask for it. They claim you can be or do anything, especially if you purchase their products or services. False optimism is their sales and marketing strategy, vague promises their stock and trade. It can seem so tempting because it plays into our fears and character defects.

We envy those teachers who outwardly appear so pretty, wealthy, and happy. And they are often the first to remind us how great they've got it—creating their effortlessly wonderful worlds, floating through life on their perfected philosophies. If we're not careful, their messages can bypass our real work, and lure us into complacency. In my case, I had caused and suffered real harm in many facets of my life. Pretending otherwise would have been silly. Acting as if I were just like everyone else would have been a lie. True optimism is based on experience, strength, and hope. Those only come with hard work, a lot of sweat and tears, countless hugs and shoulders to cry on, and an ongoing personal practice that cannot be purchased.

In my recovery, I put an attitude of kindness and gratitude above all else. That means I start with harm, rather than hope. Hope is a crucial milestone along the path to service. It is an important strategy, but for me it is not the beginning. I start with harm as a way of getting real, and to leverage truth and authenticity in order to pry myself out of despair. Only then can I create the real hope for which I long; a hope that is based in reality, and sustains me.

I start with harm because that is what leads me to action. Acknowledging all that was done to me, and owning all that I did, continually motivates me to grow, deepen, and progress. I start with harm so I can share and inspire trusted loved ones; so that I feel seen, heard, and at long last might be joined in my experience. I start with harm to come from a place of vulnerability and authenticity, such that I might build credibility and trust, in an effort to connect with something larger than myself: the harm others have suffered and are suffering. This allows me to build a solid platform from which to serve. There is no better way to get to kindness and gratitude than rigorously examining the depths to which I have sunk and the reality from which I came.

I am not a pessimist. If I truly believed the worst about people, places, and things, then it is unlikely I ever would have sought help in the first place. I would have locked myself away in solitude. God knows I tried. Today I am actually filled with hard-won hope and consumed with love. But I will not sugarcoat my experience to appease anyone. It is a matter of my personal integrity, and my story is not up for debate.

As a survivor, I have a finely honed dishonesty detector. I can sense someone's mask a mile away. This is nothing I take pride in. Unfortunately, part of my story has been searching for the hypocrisy and character defects of others, so I could use that information against them. I have spent years learning how to drop my gaze. To let others be who they are, how they are, and where they are. I first learned how to do this in 12 Step meetings. There it was routine to lead with our toughest truths, to risk everything at each meeting, and then come together in fellowship; to hug and hold hands with people from all walks of life. In doing so, we celebrate our successes and acknowledge our frailties, and finally get real, perhaps for the very first time.

It has become fashionable lately to deride 12 Step programs. This is just silly. I have personally experienced the prom-ises of the 12 Steps and have witnessed them come to life in many others. But don't take my word for it. I encourage you to be ruthlessly pragmatic about your personal growth and development. Do whatever works. But whatever you do, keep honesty and self-reflection at your core. Many of the complaints I hear about the 12 Steps involve it being "too depressing," "too religious," or "too cultish." But often this is just another way of saying its members are not pretty enough, rich enough, straight enough, white enough, or male enough, or that you think you can do it alone.

By all means, if the 12 Steps program is not for you, try something different. But just be honest about your reasons, because there are no excuses for avoiding this work. If you have been privileged enough to have the opportunity, means, and desire to change your life, it is imperative you gird yourself and move forward. Whatever method or modality you choose likely matters very little. Just do your research, pick something, and commit to it daily.

12 Step meetings are free. They have no leaders, and there is nobody to save you. You have to learn to live life by yourself, to stand on your own within the arms of the group, and to give yourself over to something larger than yourself. My dignity is too precious to further someone's ego. If as a personal growth and development expert you are unwilling to share your story, I am unwilling to listen to whatever else you might have to say. I'm also leery of guarantees. Nobody has a wisdom so expansive that they can "guarantee" their products and services will work for any specific person or situation.

There are many hucksters out there who have a vested financial interest in making us feel small. The math works something like this: You happen across an expert's book, article, seminar, etc. You learn all sorts of concepts, but for some reason, you leave with less self-worth than when you started. So you read another book, watch another video, or maybe even speak directly to the expert. You learn even more, but you come away feeling horrible about yourself. Clearly if it's not working, you must be doing something wrong. So you purchase more and more of their products and services, yet feel worse and worse about yourself. And then one day, hopefully, you realize that they are the hero of all their own stories. While you thought you were humbling yourself before someone else's wisdom, you were actually just handing over your power and agency.

If you think you might be working with this type of person, ask yourself these questions:

- When was the last time they shared something explicitly vulnerable, embarrassing, or shameful for the furtherance of their (or someone else's) spiritual growth and development?
- After you engage with this person's products and services, do you feel more or less connected to something larger than yourself?
- When you spend time with this person, do you feel more or less grounded in who you truly are?

Look, this work is not easy; it is often quite painful. You might feel sad or angry afterwards. But amidst that anguish, you should also be filled with a deeper, resonating truth. It's called "work" for a reason. Beware anyone who promises you quick fixes. If the richness of life is in the journey, and the adventure is in the unknown, why would you even want any shortcuts? I believe in the power of positive thinking, but that positivity must be authentic and real. You are fooling nobody by pretending to be someone other than yourself. By slapping on a smile on the outside when you're crying inside, you're sharing only what's pretty and nice, and denying yourself the opportunity to be who you really are.

Authentic, positive thoughts guarantee nothing. They are simply a sane response to the call of our highest purpose in the face of reality. When we say hope is a strategy, we mean that it is a lever to lift us into action. It is a means to an end, but not the end itself. The end is our service work for others, the ultimate expression of hope, and the logical outcome of kindness and gratitude. But even service work is a practice. In fact it's usually a laborious practice. The reward for hard work is more work. But that's okay because the only way to keep something is to give it away, over and over, for fun and for free, and with whatever grace we might muster in the moment.

GETTING REAL ABOUT HONESTY

I do not believe that everything happens for a reason. Actually I believe everything happens for lots of reasons, many of which are completely unseen and out of our control. We swim in a sea of powerful forces that shape all of our lives. Before we are even conceived, there are sometimes decades of intergenerational trauma absorbed in the bodies and minds of our families. In utero, we are at the mercy of our mothers' health and wellness. As small children, we are helpless to the whims of our families, which is to say nothing about the forces of our society and culture at large.

To be exposed to the forces of society is not to be subjugated by them. We need not forever be at their mercy. As adults we can observe them, acknowledge them, and move on. We have the freedom of choice. We can choose our thoughts, reactions, and feelings. We can embody our best attitudes. The truth is, we can take anything and use it to open our hearts more deeply, which I find incredibly empowering.

Here is a list of some of the subtle yet powerful forces at play in all our lives:

- **Fate:** what is done to us.
- **Fortune:** what is done for us.
- **Work:** what is done by us.
- **Reputation:** what we are known to do.
- **Fame:** what we are celebrated in doing.
- **Destiny:** what we are meant to do.
- **Karma:** what we must do.
- **Permission:** what we are allowed to do.
- **Opportunity:** what we might do.
- **Ability:** what we can do.
- **Aptitude:** what we are good at doing.
- **Affinity:** what we like to do.
- **Love:** what we long to do.
- **Calling:** what we need to do.
- **Desire:** what we want to do.
- **Aversion:** what we don't want to do.
- **Disgust:** what we hate is done.
- **Hope:** what we want to be done.
- **Fear:** what we're afraid might be done.
- **Faith:** what we believe will be done.
- **Choice:** what we decide to do.
- **Intention:** what we mean to do.
- **Resolution:** what we promise to do.
- **Dharma:** what we do.

- **Accomplishment:** what we did.
- **Regret:** what we wish we had done.

Sometimes life really sucks, and maybe you've made some horrible choices. I know I sure have. Maybe you've experienced some pretty awful things; we probably all have. But unfortunately, many of us spend a good chunk of each day lying to one another. "How are you doing?" "Fine," we respond, even though we only got four hours of sleep last night. "How is your spouse?" "Good," we say, even though we've been fighting all week. We also lie to ourselves: "I don't have a drinking problem; I just like to unwind after work," we say. Even though we can't remember the last time we skipped the bar after leaving the office. "I'm hardly eating a thing. I don't know why I'm gaining weight," we say, even though we know full well that we haven't been accurately counting our calories or correctly weighing ourselves.

These little lies, which seem so innocuous, bind many of us to a life we no longer recognize, and that's out of sync with our true purpose. They keep us from unlocking our potential. If you want to change your life, get curious. Get curious about what you're telling yourself, what you're holding back, where you're self-censoring. Listen to the words that leave your mouth. Monitor the thoughts that reside in your mind. Be rigorously honest with yourself:

- Does your thinking reflect your highest integrity?
- Do your words reflect your highest integrity?
- Do your actions reflect your highest integrity?
- How might you bring more of your truest self to all of your interactions?

Our lies often start with the distorted thinking of our family programming. In some cases, the first lie our family ever told us was that we are less than we think, and that the world is out to get us. Acceptance of this lie leaves us powerless to whichever character defects they may have weaponized and whatever cruelty they may have mustered to make themselves feel powerful. The truth is that there are all sorts of dangers in the world, but few of them are actively conspiring against us. In other cases, our families told us that we were special and that the world would fall at our feet in adoration. When that inevitably did not happen, we fell and we fell hard. Even if each of us is unique, none of us are special. And the world reminds us of that daily.

All families have family programming, which they write into the template of our lives. No matter how wonderful our childhood, we still experience this family programming today. Much of that can be righteous and empowering. You need not discard it all. And yet because there are no perfect people, there are no perfect families, and thus no perfect family programming. That means much of our personal growth and development practice involves the examination of these messages. We must ask ourselves which of these messages still serve us and which still hinder us. When we rewrite the negative messages, we are better able to integrate into the world. Just because we have the programming, does not make us beholden to it. We are not victims; we have the power to change.

Self-reflection and honesty are also the basis of morality, that collection of personal principles that helps each of us distinguish right from wrong. So many of us are at the mercy of our deluded, self-serving thinking that we have lost all touch with any semblance of a moral code, if we even had one to begin with. We might give lip service to altruism, gratitude, and intimacy without really risking anything. That means many of us need to start over, which likely also means asking for help. We must do something radically different, no matter how small, in order to shock ourselves awake. To draw a line in the sand and establish a new normal.

The pull of habitual thinking is just too strong for most of us to go it alone. Asking for help can come in many forms, but I prefer to hire experts. Our friends enhance our lives. They share our adventures and richness. They are not there to flip on life's light switches or serve as armchair psychologists. Our families are there to walk with us through the entire arc of our lives, love us even during those moments in which they may not like us, and hold our entire story. They are not there to solve our problems. That would be debilitating. Sure, friends and family might lend a loving ear from time to time, when they can. But if we're really serious about making changes to improve our lives, we will most likely need to hire paid professionals with experience, training, and neutrality. These experts can devote undivided attention to our stories, offer perspective, and hold us accountable.

GETTING REAL ABOUT TALK THERAPY

Clawing my way out of the shadows took years of hard work. I invested thousands of hours and dollars in my personal growth. My case might be extreme, but on some level, I realized that the only thing more painful than making this investment would be *not* making this investment. Even though I had no idea where all that time and money would come from, in the end I had no choice. My mind was spiraling out of control. It was clear I did not have the skills, education, or experience to save myself. I would have to hire a team of experts and just trust that the means to pay for them would come. And somehow, at each step of the journey, I found a way. Through a combination of grace, luck, privilege, hard work, and the generosity of loved ones, everything seemed to fall into place. So I gathered myself, marshaled my resources, and dove in. I put everything I had into this project of recovery. And while the cost was high, I shudder to think where I might otherwise be, had I chosen differently.

I first started this process in talk therapy. Over the course of fifteen years, I have worked with several different therapists. I picked up the process for a few years and then set it down again as I became full and required rest and time to implement all I had learned. I was fortunate to find therapists I trusted and adored. I encourage you to be pragmatic about picking a therapist. There are so many types of therapy out there, and so many different types of therapists. Don't settle for just good enough! Find someone who inspires you, whom you want to emulate, and whose life is part of your goal. Each therapist I hired spent months on the intake process, learning about my life, and documenting my version of my story, so we could work together to rewrite it.

It turns out I had to rewrite my story in order to create an identity, one based on my truth rather than the accumulated messages I absorbed along the way. I used to dwell in the past, mired in a morass of regret. But once my therapists helped me thoughtfully examine the actual events and context of my experience, I was able to craft a personal narrative, one that had a beginning and an ending. What had once seemed insurmountable turned out to be rather mild, or at least not so all-encompassing. Even the horrible events I had experienced and the awful choices I made were finite. They could not eclipse the vastness of my spirit, or preclude the fullness of my redemption. But it was my mind that wanted to keep me stuck, to wallow in the safe and familiar.

I rewrote my story in order to build new neurological connections in my brain, and to recontextualize everything I thought I knew about myself. I mean this literally: I actually wrote words to reclaim my life, and those words became my medicine. Over the years, I've come to see the brain as an anxiety-inducing organ of fight or flight. It is determined to avoid conflict and protect our bodies, as well as help negotiate our way through the world. Our brains are also organs of thought. They receive stimuli from the outside world, so that they might control the body and project the mind. While the brain is a physical organ, the mind transcends the body into the realm of thought and imagination. The mind associates and categorizes information, and uses language to create stories, all in the name of survival. These stories form the basis of personality (our likes, dislikes, aptitudes, and affinities) and identity (our values, ideals, and guiding principles). Put together, these facets of the mind comprise our worldview and become an entry point into connecting with others, which is what it's all about. The mind is fundamental to human design, such that there is no health without mental health. These new stories we tell ourselves about our lives become our cure and the best way to protect our minds.

GETTING REAL ABOUT PSYCHIATRIC MEDICATION

After working with a therapist for a sustained period, you might decide to complement that work with a course of pharmaceutical medications, in order to help balance your brain chemistry. Your therapist can help point you in the right direction, but if possible, I highly encourage you to establish a baseline of health and wellness prior to beginning any new pharmaceutical regimen. This means reducing or removing all alcohol and recreational drug consumption, lowering your caffeine intake, improving your nutrition, ensuring you get enough rest, and implementing a physical fitness program. While it's important not to let the perfect be the enemy of the good, establishing this baseline before adding any new medications to your body will ensure their success.

Many of us require medication, through no fault of our own, in order to live our lives. There is absolutely no shame in this. It is not a moral issue at all. Some of this is due to structural issues in our brains, other areas of our bodies, or even our lived experiences. If you are already on medication, please consult with your healthcare professional prior to altering your program in any way. In some cases, if we choose not to continue with a specific medication, we must slowly ween ourselves off of it with the help of a professional, in order to avoid nasty side effects. Likewise, if your symptoms are such that you must stop your medications immediately, please work with a healthcare professional to chart the best course of action for you.

Consult your full team of medical professionals in order to review all potential side effects of any new medication before you begin a course of treatment. Your body is a complex system that is unique to you. Many of these drugs are powerful agents and can have side effects and unintended consequences, particularly if you have other health issues or are currently taking other medications. While a psychiatrist can help you pick the right drug, your primary care physician can ensure this medication will not have adverse consequences with any other medications or medical issues.

The rest of your healthcare professionals will be incredibly useful for their different points of view, based on their various areas of expertise. Each will bring a unique piece of information to the table. They will want to know any drugs you introduce into your system, as they continue to monitor your overall health and wellness. Medications can be a fantastic way to create a foundation for you to advance your mental health, but they are not quick fixes. Once you stabilize your brain chemistry, you are still left with all the issues that got you here in the first place. Continuing your talk therapy is a great strategy to support this process. Your therapist will continue to monitor your modes of thinking and ensure you are tethered to a strong foundation.

GETTING REAL ABOUT MEDITATION

Now that you have stabilized your brain chemistry, it is an excellent time to build a meditation practice. If you have yet to try meditation, fear not. There are a variety of ways to demystify the process. From videos to blog posts, there is a plethora of free information online. There are also numerous books on the topic. All of these are great ways to get started. But if you have the time and money, I highly recommend a meditation class. You can often find these classes available at your local yoga studio. The advantage of taking a class is that it forces you to show up in person and to forge new relationships with like-minded attendees, as well as the teacher. This gives you the opportunity to ask questions in real time and to bond with others. Most meditation classes are pay-as-you-go, but some are sold as a series, if you prefer to jump into a larger commitment. There are many forms and styles of meditation, classes, and teachers. Find the one that resonates with you. The key is to pick one and stick with it.

Many meditation practices involve sitting in silence. The advantage of these practices is that they are portable. You can do them in your house, in a studio, or in a hotel room. Some practices have you sit comfortably in a position that promotes good posture, while you close your eyes and observe your breathing. Other practices have you select a mantra that you repeat to yourself over a set period of time. A mantra is a special phrase that protects the mind; words that trigger stillness and connection to something larger than you; words that help you touch the immortal infinite, as you drop into the present moment. You can find entire books filled with mantras, or in some cases your teacher will select a mantra for you. Some meditation practices involve movement, such as tai chi or walking a spiritual labyrinth. In reality, just about anything can be a form of meditation: singing, playing a musical instrument, or even playing a sport. The key to mediation is that you rest your mind and allow the dust to settle, such that you can replenish and restore what is most uniquely you, by tapping into something larger.

Meditation can also be a great visualization tool. As you connect to the truest, deepest expression of yourself, it will be easier to manifest your mission, vision, and values over the course of your daily life and interactions. Athletes often use this technique before a big game; musicians often use it before an important performance. Honing a quiet concentration practice can have a dramatic and positive impact, whether that's in the workplace or at home. If you have an important presentation at work or anticipate a tough conversation with a client or coworker, meditation can be a great tool to ensure you present your best self. Likewise, if you anticipate drama with your spouse or child, meditation can be a great way to mentally relax and prepare. While diving into the world of meditation might seem daunting at first, there is all sorts of help. The key is that whatever practice you adopt, you quiet your mind, embrace some form of silence, and find your place in the universe.

Most of us are weary from our daily lives and fear we lack capacity for much of anything. But this fear is a lie. It starts with stillness: can we cultivate some stillness each day in order to tap into our greatest good? This stillness inevitably stokes curiosity: what could we do that's feasible, viable, and advisable? This curiosity begets creativity: how can we act asymmetrically and work indirectly, in ways that combine wants and needs, and leverage our strengths? This creativity leads to action: what strategies and tactics will lead us to our goals? What is our plan?

GETTING REAL ABOUT LIFE COACHING

After you maintain a solid baseline and stabilize your brain chemistry, I recommend you hire a life coach to round out your support team. Your therapist will help hold your story, while your coach will help you create the life of your dreams.

There are many types of life coaches, but my favorites are those with relentless honesty and pragmatism. Pick someone who can tell you what they did to get what they have. That will become your road map and the vision for the new you, which will be more you than you've ever been. Unlike talk therapy, which is typically conducted in-person, most life coaches meet with you online. So, the world is your oyster!

My life coach has helped me articulate my mission, vision, and values. He has challenged me to create a more purpose-driven life, rather than just being a passive witness to events that happen to me. The great thing about this modality is the speed at which you will see results. Talk therapy can take years to forge a relationship and experience transformation, but I started to see results with my life coach in just a few weeks, and after a few months, much of my life was unrecognizable.

Neither your therapist nor your life coach need to share your sexual orientation, sexual identification, gender identity, or gender expression. But they should either have familiarity with your community, or at least demonstrate a willingness and propensity to learn. My current therapist is a straight, cisgendered, younger man. But I don't hold that against him! I trust and adore him. It might be that I am the only openly gay person he has ever known, but it wouldn't matter. He has demonstrated so much loving kindness and compassion over the years that I know I'm in good hands. He meets me where I am and treats me as a whole person. I've been working with him for five years and, over time, have reduced the frequency of our sessions to a couple of times each month. I look forward to these sessions and can't imagine my life without them.

My life coach on the other hand is a bisexual, cisgendered, younger man who lives halfway around the world! But through the magic of the internet, we are able to maintain daily contact and weekly one-on-one sessions. Even though both men are much younger than me, I look up to them. I decided long ago that I wasn't going to let the messenger distract me from the message. The point is to create space for the universe to work its wonders. Don't let the identities of loved ones prevent them from helping you, if they are truly willing to meet you where you are and see the real you.

GETTING REAL ABOUT FALLING IN LOVE WITH YOUR MIND

It's no secret that technology is evolving faster than our minds, much less our culture. We are so inundated with information that we have become lost in decision fatigue. We have forgotten how to create space and savor the free-dom associated with boredom. Boredom is that mental state of nothingness, the absence of thought. If there is an inhale and an exhale to life, boredom exists at the end of the exhalation, just before the breath rushes back in. Boredom pushes us forward to reach for the world, to learn, grow, and play. It is the mother of the curiosity that leads to dreams and goals.

It's tough to love a mind that races and rages. That means as part of your personal growth and development journey, you will likely need to cease many of your former thought patterns. You will have to set some things down that you have become used to carrying, and let go of old stories that you have long embraced. You must change the messages in your mind, so you can change the way you think and speak. It will alter what the world experiences when it experiences you.

Most of us need a team to support the stabilizing of our brain chemistry and the healing of our minds. There is absolutely no shame here. In this day and age, it is common for people to coordinate their mental health with their primary care physician, therapist, psychiatrist, life coach, and others. Our bodies are complex systems, and many of us require a team of specialists to approach the various structures of our mental health: the brain, the mind, and the ways in which we relate to ourselves and others. I simply was not able to do this on my own. It was just too easy to be consumed by the day-to-day activities of running my life, and too easy to lose the forest for the trees.

I realized that the life story I adopted from the world and my family was keeping me stuck. The self-destructive sound bites running through my head on a daily basis were lulling me to sleep, such that I might lock myself away from the world, fortified in a bunker of safety and seclusion, and my mind might finally know peace. But this was a false peace. Torpor in lieu of growth, security at the expense of freedom—the freedom to unleash my mind and unlock my true potential. It is a freedom made possible by years of investments and hard work, supported on the shoulders of experts and in the arms of loved ones. Loved ones who would walk with me, laugh with me, and let my mind finally run free.

SUMMARY

Our minds are the projected transcendent form of our

brains, that part of us responsible for thought and imagination. Our brain receives information from the outside world and uses our mind to convert that information into insights and stories, which build culture and help us survive. But if left unchecked, our family programming can easily intercede and distort our thinking. Eventually these distortions can become lies: falsehoods we tell ourselves and one another in order to ease our discomfort and anxiety but, ultimately, entrap us. Cultivating a healthy attitude involves honestly facing our lives, taking stock, and owning our actions as well as our choices. There is no shortcut to kindness and gratitude. We must do the work.

Most of us require the help of paid professionals to support our journey into a purpose-driven life. These experts can help us retrain our minds, implement self-care programs, or even prescribe the psychiatric medications to stabilize our brain chemistry. Our friends and family are unqualified to walk with us through each phase of this journey. That is not their role. They've got their own lives to lead and journeys to walk.

Many talk therapists will spend months with you, extensively examining and holding the story of your life, helping you contextualize your history, and applying a sense of proportion to it. During this process, it might become clear that a certain course of psychiatric medication is warranted to help stabilize your brain chemistry. Your therapist can refer you to a psychiatrist who can help assess the situation and prescribe a course of medication that is right for you. Life coaches on the other hand are here to help us manifest our dreams. They help us create a purpose-driven life by articulating our mission, vision, and values. A life coach also helps you pinpoint perceived obstacles, and then plow through them. At the end of the day, our team will help us work hard to return to love. A love of our stories and ourselves. A love of our minds, such that we might serve each other and light up the world.

CHAPTER 3

SPIRIT

I am an atheist. Which is another way of saying I put my faith in the here and now. I believe in the present moment, rather than whatever came before or might come next. Faith is belief in the absence of evidence, and I have faith in many things. I believe in the power of the human spirit and the brilliance of the human mind. My prayers are an attempt to invoke our better natures, rather than messages to some all-knowing being. While I believe that bodies of superior power and intelligence inhabit this universe, I do not believe there is a grand architect, much less one that requires, or even wants, our supplication. Some might call this brand of faith "secular humanism," but for me the label is unnecessary. It's just what I believe.

In my spiritual journey, I have sat with Quakers and Buddhists, and I have stood with Lutherans and Episcopalians, yet I do not feel part of any particular movement, nor any group-oriented faith-based practice. In this way, I am connected to everybody, which is another way of saying that there is nowhere to hide. Everyone is my soulmate, and we are all in this together. Maybe someday I will join others. Find a spiritual home that celebrates the innate goodness of all things, understands the beauty of radical inclusion, and teaches the value of continuity with an eye toward opportunity. I would share that home with all who enter, such that we might raise our voices and sing of togetherness. But today, I practice alone.

I come from a Christian family, and have experienced Christian abuse. My family questioned, shamed, and ridiculed my sexuality and gender expression, until they forced me in the closet completely—all in the name of Jesus. But even worse was that, as a child, the spark of my nascent spirituality was left entirely unlit, and the wisdom I should have acquired through ceremonies, initiations, and rites of passage was never transmitted. I earned my insight exclusively through lived experience, unnecessary tragedy, and heartbreak. Perhaps my secularism is a response to the vile behavior I witnessed: the shaming of souls, the othering of neighbors and loved ones, the consolidation of power in a select few, as well as the homogeneity of narrowmindedness, usually bound by race, gender, and sexual orientation. Yes, in churches I have also witnessed tender mercies, true selflessness, and love writ large. One does not obviate the other. Harm can be amended, but never undone. Our words and actions are sacred. Even wrongs made right are never truly unwritten, no matter how much honor there might be in the effort.

We must start with the harm, and the harm has been legion: Christians have tortured and killed gay men for centuries. They have cast us out of their families and communities, and rendered us helpless and hopeless. We have been laughed at, spit upon, imprisoned, institutionalized, physically and chemically castrated, psychologically tortured, and forced to choose between quiet desperation and public humiliation. At long last, the church recently awoke to find itself as part of a shrinking cultural minority. Some organizations split between those who wanted better, and those who wanted worse. Some members left for greener pastures; others were driven out. Meanwhile, those who remained consolidated their ugly power. Bigotry is a relentless process of purification—a distillation through prejudice and certainty. This cycle whittles away all we thought we knew, until what's left is a circular firing squad and the ugly mirror of our personal self-loathing.

As we grow accustomed to our privilege and power, it is tempting to lie to ourselves: we are good people, have a well-meaning congregation, and would never intentionally harm anyone. But if we are members of a well-meaning church that promises inclusion, yet does not explicitly celebrate gay lives and bodies, then we are condoning, or even participating in, spiritual abuse. If we belong to a church that does not embody equality by conducting gay weddings and celebrating gay marriages, we are part of the problem. If our church has no openly gay priests, preachers, or officers, it is a house of bigotry. If our congregation does not hold up gay families, it is participating in child abuse. It is all too easy to pat ourselves on the backs while sitting in the cheap seats, pretending we love everyone—to put up rainbow flags and send a few parishioners to Gay Pride events, without risking anything and never truly leaving our comfort zone.

If we truly want to be a house of inclusion, we've got to get real. We've got to own the actions of our ancestors, along with the intergenerational trauma that has become our collective inheritance. If we want to extend our hands in caritas, then we must get in the fight. We must go somewhere that frightens us, and challenges our delicate sensibilities. We must leverage our privilege for the benefit of those less advantaged. For many of us, that will require risking more than what's comfortable. But let's ask ourselves this: just how loudly are we willing to love? To those gay men who might be part of such congregations, it's time for some rigorous honesty. Are we truly working within the system to foster it on behalf of all people? Or are we staying cozy, garnering crumbs of proximal power from those who have a vested financial incentive in oppression?

The fact that humans regularly fall short of their highest values is not news. Those who hold themselves in high esteem have long tried to obliterate gay men; this is well-documented. But what we rarely discuss is the marked absence of any sort of spiritual replacement for our community. We who barely escaped with our lives, and lost so many brothers along the way, have long sought refuge in lesser places, such as safe solitude, illicit substances, and rampant sex. In many ways, that's what a spiritual practice is: where we seek refuge. When things get tough, where do we turn? And what does our practice yield? Does it connect us to something larger than ourselves? Does it sustain us throughout the arc of our lives? Or is it just a quick fix to mask our pain? What does our refuge cost? Our friends, our families, our relationships, our jobs? If the costs of our spiritual practice outweigh the benefits, maybe it's time to make a change.

Some might feel called to fight for change in existing places of worship. Others might want to change churches, or leave their current system of faith entirely. But the key is we all have options. As gay men, we are not beholden to their stories about us. We get to find our own way and chart our own path. So it's time we get both informed and empowered. These days there are many genuinely welcoming and affirming churches, sanctuaries, synagogues, and houses of worship. There is also a wealth of information at our fingertips to help support our personal spiritual practices. Our spirituality can be based on whatever we choose. We need not wait for the apologies or amends of others. We need not suffer in silence or slink in the shadows. We can create our own seat at the table or build a new table altogether.

There is no hope without spirituality. The cards are simply too stacked against us. Hope is our best strategy to stave off fear, anger, and weariness. Fortunately, hope and spirituality are available to all of us, even atheists. Spirit is entirely separate from religious organization or affiliation, and does not necessarily imply faith in the divine. For me, spirituality is a concept that connects me to my best self and my highest good—that part of me without ego, which longs to serve. My current spiritual practice is based on various principles associated with loving kindness. The daily work of taking care of my body, creating space to clear my mind, actively seeing the best in my loved ones, and giving until it hurts. I practice taking the time to rule people in, rather than rule them out. I practice remembering that relatedness is my primary reason for just about everything. I practice cultivating an active and abiding love for this planet and celebrating the persistent mysteries of the universe. The whole point of my practice is service and generosity—honoring all that I have been given by giving it all away. Such is the chain of life, passing from one person to the next, a web of love and intrinsic interconnectedness.

GETTING REAL ABOUT PHYSICAL FITNESS

If you are struggling to create your own spiritual practice, start concentrating on daily engagement with your body. Whatever your beliefs, we are each of us having a physical experience on this planet, so it is essential to start there. Examine your nutrition and physical fitness. What are you putting into your body? How are you reducing belly fat and building/toning muscle? Regardless of your physical fitness goals, having a healthy body is an essential part of your spiritual practice. A baseline of health will ensure you have the energy and vitality to truly serve your greatest good.

In order to optimize your physical health:

- Create a nutrition plan to ensure you avoid as many synthetic substances as possible.
- Count your calories to optimize your portion sizes during mealtimes.
- Eat only when you are hungry, to cut down on idle snacking.
- Work with your healthcare professional to measure your testosterone levels. If necessary, select natural supplements that will safely boost your testosterone, as well as support muscle and joint health.
- Stabilize your sleep routine.
- Find ways to incorporate daily cardiovascular and resistance training.

There is so much information out there, so remember to

consult with your healthcare professionals and hire experts to help you along the way.

As we address the needs of our bodies, most of us would do well to spend more time in nature. Not only is it essential to breathe the clean air of the outdoors, but the sights and sounds will stir our souls. We will inevitably feel small, as we are surrounded by a power greater than our own. The more immersive this experience, the better. This way we can truly lose ourselves, stoke our sense of gratitude, and reemerge with a sense of being part of a larger whole.

We need not go to the wilds of Alaska to enjoy nature. There are beautiful natural settings just about everywhere. Most urban landscapes contain parks, lakes, and rivers. Even many suburbs have designated green spaces. Spending time in nature can involve any number of activities: camping, hiking, walking, gardening, picnics, exercise, work, play, etc. The key is to leave technology and the demands of modern life behind, if only for a short while, so that we can nourish our souls and remember who we were meant to be. There simply is no substitute for the natural world. It is where we belong and what we belong to. It is our home.

Movement is a key component of body work. I recommend incorporating systems like dance, yoga, tai chi, or Pilates into your routine. These modalities more explicitly bridge the gap between the physical world and the spiritual plane. By combining breath work, chanting, and meditation techniques with physical movement, you will quiet your mind and deepen your experience of you. You will more fully realize the interconnectedness intrinsic to the web of life. Not all body work need be active. Massage and acupuncture are great ways to both heal and nurture your body, as well as connect to a deeper part of yourself. From the Alexander Technique to Rolfing, there are numerous other restorative, passive body work modalities that can help foster better alignment, release the buildup of muscle toxins, and promote your overall well-being. As always, you are in charge. You get to decide what works for you.

It is essential to make time each day to tune out the external world and reconnect with your true self. That part of you separate from your various masks and roles. That part of you which has nothing to do with your job function or your cash flow, which does not own or owe a thing, which is both uniquely you, yet cut from a larger cloth. The part of you that is somehow both ineffable and banal, immovable yet ethereal. There is nothing more elemental than your relationship with your body, and there is no more effective messenger than your body. It is the bridge between your spirit and the natural world. Any investment you make in nurturing or healing your body will also intrinsically support your soul.

GETTING REAL ABOUT MEDITATION

I recommend extending the depth of your body awareness to your mind by engaging with others, both in person and through literature. Mental stimulation is requisite to a full life, and the brain is stimulated by conflict. It wants to be challenged, in the same way your body wants to be exercised. Not only can activities such as learning new languages, travelling, or reading books challenge your assumptions, but they also help create new neural pathways. They stoke our humility and remind us of our innate smallness, so we connect with an inner reverence: that which we hold dear and treat with deep, abiding respect. This space is called meditation. Meditation is any state in which you exercise your mental acuity, such that you can shed your sense of self, while experiencing both the nothingness and the everythingness of the universe.

Over time those ideas, objects, and practices actually become sacred, imbued with a deeper meaning than their face value. The only thing that separates the sacred from the profane is the manner in which we hold it—the connectedness to some larger purpose and power that it provides. In this way, anything can be sacred. You can experience the same sacredness at the gym as in a yoga class, in your home as in nature, in a school as in a church. What matters is you and your approach. What are you also holding when you hold that experience? How does that practice lift you up and elevate the intrinsic banality of life? All that really needs to shift is our attitude. This means our practice is portable: we can do it anywhere. There is no place that is untouched by the sacred, no person immune from benevolence. Each of us has the power to bestow kindness and gratitude, to touch the world with light, and to acknowledge all that we encounter while loving what is.

Long ago, many of our ancestors adorned themselves in talismans and built totems to reflect and harness the power of nature. These were not just pretty jewelry and empty symbols. Our ancestors understood the inherent sacredness in everyday objects blessed with intention. They used these objects to train their minds and remember themselves of their deepest truth: that there is no separation between themselves, the natural world, and the spiritual plane. It is all one; we are all one. They knew from their lived experience that we are all in this together. That to survive means to join and to live means to embrace. They believed that the afterlife is a place of reunion, with both the source and all we thought we had lost. For them, being cast out of society was a fate worse than death; it violated every natural and spiritual law. Spiritual and physical togetherness were the same thing, and it can be so for us, too. We can create our own talismans and totems. They can be anything, from the simple to the ornate, from the handcrafted to the purchased. Objects are objects—the key is the blessing. You can perform this blessing yourself, or ask a spiritual friend or mentor. There are no rules, other than maintaining an open heart and an empty mind.

Once you have acquired your spiritual objects, use them wisely. Each time you hold them, hold them dear. See through the literal object to the original blessing. If you wear them, wear them with wise words. Take a moment as you dress to say the associated prayer. Visualize your original intention. Unite your mind with the object. If you use these objects in your spiritual practice, then lock some of them away to preserve their power. Other objects can sit uncovered throughout your home or office, so that you randomly encounter them over the course of the day. They will smile upon you and remind you of your truest self. They will jolt you out of the mundane, lift you above the banal, and enrich your day. Again, there are no rules. You are completely in charge. These objects are spiritual because you make them spiritual. Don't let anyone else tell you otherwise or intercede uninvited.

GETTING REAL ABOUT PLAY

Play is the most spiritual thing any of us can do. It is the liberating union of mind, body, and spirit. It is essential to mammalian brain development, as well as the building and cementing of social networks. As adults, many of us lose this ability. We tell ourselves that we lack the requisite time and energy, or that our play is just a waste of time. But the truth is just the opposite. It is imperative that we all take time to experience joy as manifested through silly, harmless play. Say something stupid. Embarrass yourself. Look like a fool. Don't underestimate the power of this joyful humility. For those of us with control issues and the need to protect our self-images, play can be our deepest spiritual work.

Art is the highest form of play and the most quintessential of human activities. It is unique to us and at the core of our humanity. Anthropologists can confirm the existence of humans when they find evidence of art. To engage with art is to be fully human. We need not be Rembrandt or Bach. We can engage with art by going to a museum, attending a concert, or going to the theatre. Witnessing live art nourishes the soul, but I encourage you to incorporate the doing of art into your spiritual practice as well. You need not be talented or educated to reap the rewards. You need not inflict your artistic experiments, trials, and errors on the world in order to experience the benefits. The key is to let your spirit fly free.

In order to freely engage in play, many of us will have to cultivate a connection with our inner children. In my case, I spent my childhood trying to survive. I was never taught how to play, or even afforded the capacity. So I had to go back and join that little boy, in order to heal a core wound.

That inner bonding has involved talk therapy, reading, and coaching. But most importantly, it has involved envisioning and sitting with that hurt little boy, and then explicitly communicating with him all that he needs to hear, in order to move on.

Here's a love letter that I (as an adult) wrote to my inner child:

> Do you remember that time we built a bunker in the woods? And you promised to protect me from this brutal world? You said they could not kill what they could not catch, and your anger was old, old, old.
>
> In all these years, you never let the legions storm the castle, or gave up watch throughout the night. You taught me that there is no love without courage or character, and that to harness my power I need just occupy the throne.
>
> Now you may rest, little prince, sweetly tucked away inside the keep, where you shall always reside, young and free. Or when come out to play, running through flowers and green fields, safe in the knowledge that you are cherished and adored.

It might seem silly at first, but writing letters like these can have a surprisingly profound effect on parts of you that you rarely access. Turn off your mind, get creative, put pen to paper, and just let your spirit speak through you.

Lastly, cultivate your commitment to your values by regularly engaging them. If you are committed to kindness, then practice kindness. If you are committed to humility, then practice humility. For me, this is what it means to pray. It is less a matter of asking for extrinsic help from an all-knowing being, than realizing that I already have all the benevolence I need. I just might require a reminder each day through action. The prayer is in the doing of things, not the requesting of them. By putting my attitude into action through serving others, I become inspired. My actions lead me to my divine guidance, which reminds me of my true identity and intrinsic worth. It pulls into focus all that I am, and all that I am not. Through serving others, I touch our complex web of interconnectedness, which I call "heaven" and is with me to experience each day, right here, right now.

GETTING REAL ABOUT SELF-FORGIVENESS

Through serving others, I practice living amends and the forgiveness of myself. Forgiveness of others is something children do to heal, secure, and foster relatedness. Except in the extreme cases, forgiveness is not an advanced spiritual practice. It's actually quite simple. The heart longs for it to happen; all we need do is get out of the way. Forgiving ourselves is a choice adults make to acknowledge our past transgressions and hold the fact that we are not now who we once were. We have grown, evolved, apologized, and made amends. We are thus redeemed.

To withhold forgiveness of ourselves is an act of self-aggrandizement. It is a way to stay stuck in our negative love patterns and self-fulfilling prophecies. It is a way of proclaiming that nobody has ever been where we once were, has ever experienced our level of suffering, or inflicted our amount of harm. This is just silly. There is nothing we can say, or do, or think, or feel that removes us from redemption, precludes our self-forgiveness, or warrants our exclusion. Plenty have been where we were, and plenty more will one day find themselves there as well. Self-forgiveness is an extension of the forgiveness of others.

If you struggle with self-forgiveness, I suggest you try laughter. It is impossible to laugh at yourself while overthinking things. It is impossible to laugh at yourself with an inflated ego. Laughing at yourself is the convergence of humility and joy. There is something about the physical act of laughter that releases tension and eases the mind. And when that energy is directed inwards, at our own lives, it becomes a tonic to hate and small-mindedness. That's why there are entire spiritual practices built solely around the healing properties of laughter. Here is a practice that has worked for me:

- Write down all those transgressions that continue to bind you to who you think you once were, preventing you from realizing your best self. Maybe (like me) you've caused a lot of harm and created a lot of chaos in your life. But I swear to you, the list of your wrongs will be finite. There will be a beginning and an ending to it. Chances are, when you look at it, the list will be much smaller than the vague sense of harm rattling around in your brain.
- Spend time with your list of transgressions, meditating on the larger context and systems at play which enabled or enticed you to this behavior. It is critical that you own exactly your part, no more and no less. If there are others that led you to violate your integrity, then acknowledge that, without fear or malice. Hold each person you included on your list up to the light and explicitly forgive them; release yourself and release them.
- Next to each item on your list, include a counterexam-

ple of how you act (meaning who you are) today. For instance, if you have stolen something in the past, cite present examples of your generosity and integrity. Hold each situation in your heart while you practice self-forgiveness. Remember what it felt like, back then, in those moments. Contrast that with what you feel today each time you live up to your greatest good. Verbally express your sorrow and self-forgiveness. Release yourself.

- Return to your list of transgressions. Feel the smallness and silliness of your choices, the lighthearted delusion in your thinking, as well as the disconnectedness from your true self, your loved ones, and the universe. Have a good laugh at what you thought you knew and believed at that time. This experience will inspire a sense of awe in how much you have changed. Notice your lightheartedness and observe the sense of relief in your body—how a weight has started to lift—as you set down your sack of rocks.

The entire point of this practice is to let go of who you once were, so you can more fully step into your new life. To lighten your load and free your heart, so you might embody the feeling of joy and evoke your primary purpose.

GETTING REAL ABOUT SPIRITUAL CEREMONIES

In addition to my daily spiritual practices, I also find it important to create regularly recurring ceremonies that honor the meaningful elements of each year. A ceremony is a formal celebration, a party that has become more than just a social gathering built around play. Ceremonies include elements that are explicitly spiritual. By "formal" I just mean that the events in these ceremonies are pre-planned and well-thought out. Everything is spiritual, so you can build your ceremonies around anything you want, just as long as it is meaningful to you.

One easy place to start is by marking the seasons of the year, which you can then overlay with the seasons of your life. This process will help you attune to the natural rhythms of the planet. It will also give you a nice mix of annual touch points with which you can honor something larger than yourself, as well as frequent reasons to celebrate this world and your place in it.

Over time, these ceremonies become traditions and rituals, the reenactments of our personal mythology. Our personal mythology is the collection of those stories we hold dear, that deepen our experience and connect us to greater meaning. If we do not reenact these myths, they will remain locked in our minds, disconnected from our bodies, and eventually become drained of all power.

Here are some sample ceremonies you might explore:

- **Birthdays:** In order to elevate a birthday from a party to a ceremony, put more thought into the preparation. Include various components that explicitly celebrate the spirit of the guest of honor, as well as the other attendees.
- **Anniversaries:** Instead of just doing something easy, plan an event. Even a simple dinner together can be a special event, if something thoughtful is required from each of you. We might not all have the budget for something fancy, but anyone can write a poem or create a

blessing. The point is to share from your soul, not your wallet.

- **Memorials:** When someone dies, they never truly leave us. And while we might visit them daily in our hearts and minds, creating a regularly recurring ceremony, dedicated just to them, is a wonderful way to honor the love that we shared.

- **The New Year:** While annual resolutions have become cliché, the New Year is still a natural marker for most of us to begin again, just as we begin fresh each morning after sleep. You need not do anything as contrived as aligning intentions to the calendar in order to experience the beauty of this ceremony. Perhaps you celebrate indirectly by honoring the beginner in each of us. Remember that eternal endings and beginnings mirror the exhale and inhale of our bodies and the universe.

- **Spring Equinox:** The changing of the seasons is a natural marker in the course of a year. Humans have long associated the spring season with fertility, so that's a logical place to start. What are you creating in your life, and how can you honor that? What will you use to "spring" forward?

- **Summer Solstice:** The beginning of summer has traditionally marked the midpoint of the year (a perfect time for new beginnings, within the context of a given year). It also represents the peak energy of the year, since it is the longest day. This makes it an excellent time to celebrate light. You might decide to get up early that day and greet the sunrise in some way that is meaningful to you. Or build a bonfire at dusk to honor the passing of light into dark.

- **Fall Equinox:** Of course many have long associated this season with the agrarian harvest. It is a time to reap the rewards of our labors and replenish our stores for the coming cold. What rewards will you reap? How do you intend to replenish?

- **Winter Solstice:** The first day of winter marks the longest night of the year. That makes it a natural time of quiet energy. It also marks the end of many ancient calendars. This can make it a season to look inward and celebrate the year that was and all that will be in the year ahead.
- **Travel:** Before your next trip, you might plan a goodbye and welcome home ceremony for yourself. This can be a nice way to bookend the experience, and to prepare for exit and reentry, which is often incredibly stressful. How can you focus on sweetness and gentleness to ease your transition?

It is imperative to get spiritually empowered and take ownership of your year. Your list of ceremonies will likely look different than mine. That's okay. Get creative: explore those ceremonies and naturally occurring events that have personal meaning to you.

Adding these markers to the course of your year and your life will assist your attunement. It will help you align with larger cycles than the daily vicissitudes of your mind. There is a union of the mind, body, and spirit in the ceremonies that reenact our personal mythology. The beauty is in the actual doing of them. The power of their regularity transcends the simple comfort of familiarity. They become emotional and spiritual anchors. They tether our souls to something larger than ourselves. In doing so, we remember our place in the world and embody a deeper humility.

SUMMARY

Every spiritual practice should contain aspects supporting your body, mind, and play. Your spiritual practice should also be based on your purpose, values, self-forgiveness, ceremonies, and service. It should inspire you to manifest all that you hold dear and bolster your best self. Think of it as nourishment for your soul: that deepest, most constant part of you. As a member of the gay community, people have most assuredly sought us harm. They tried to manipulate, control, hurt, and even kill us. But today most of us are safe. We are adults who have the power and freedom to build a spirituality that serves our greatest good, the capacity to honor what's real, and the strength to feed our souls.

When it comes to creating your personal spiritual practice, the key is that you are in the driver's seat. It's up to you to take ownership. Nobody is going to do it for you, and you should not allow anybody to do it to you. Your spiritual practice is yours and yours alone, regardless of whether you practice in solitude or in community. You own it. You are responsible for the maintenance, management, and results. That means if it's not working, change it. There are no rules, other than aligning with your values and connecting with something larger than your own ego.

When you assess your success, ask yourself, "How efficiently and effectively am I serving others?" Spirituality without service invariably becomes self-indulgent and unsustainable. It is through service that we manifest humility and acknowledge our limitations. It is through service that we know interdependency, and learn to love and be loved. It is through service that we are healed and made whole, and nobody can take that away from us. It is ours alone to give.

CHAPTER 4

CAREER

Graduating with a fine arts degree means always having to say you're sorry, over and over again, as you encounter questions from friends and loved ones, strangers and coworkers. You try to explain your field of study and justify your life choices, while they just shake their heads, looking longingly in the distance for any possible off-ramp. I found out the hard way that being a poet and flutist gives you a quick way to stop any conversation in its tracks, but also means many people won't take you seriously.

Nobody will hold your hand and help you build a career; you must figure it out for yourself. When I completed graduate school, I had no idea what to do. It was quickly becoming clear that I was not going to be able to earn the type of living I desired in my fields of study. To make matters worse, I had no marketable skills, at least in the eyes of prospective employers. But by some incredible stroke of luck, I happened to be living in Seattle during the dot-com boom at the turn of the century, when anyone with a pulse could get a job. And a pulse was just about all I had going for me.

Somehow I found an employment agency that was willing to take a chance on me. Who knows why? I'm sure I was punctual, and hopefully I smiled. I had a glowing reference from a former arts colleague, which by some miracle sufficed, and just like that, my career in information technology (IT) was born. This was almost entirely due to luck: the privilege of my identity combined with the great fortune of applying for work during a period of relatively full employment. I remember sitting at my desk on the very first day of my very first job. I thought to myself, "Okay. I can do this. Maybe even for the next twenty years. I'm going to be okay." I worked as hard as I could over the next few months, and then slowly but surely, something completely unexpected happened: I realized I was good at it. I mean really good at it.

Somehow everything just clicked. I guess all those years spent studying classical music paid off. Thousands of hours spent practicing scales and etudes, hundreds of performances for all sorts of audiences, all while systematically (even obsessively) analyzing my strengths and weaknesses. But my secret, untapped talents did not end there. All those poems and analytical essays I wrote at university taught me to crank out a position statement like nobody's business. All those hours spent teaching in the classroom and in private lessons taught me to break down difficult concepts into bite-sized chunks. It turned out my fine arts degree *was* my secret weapon!

Those skills I cultivated as an artist, seamlessly applied

to the risk analysis skills required of any IT professional. What I never could have planned was that, thanks to the newly tapped powers of the internet, the surprising confluence of marketing and technology was just beginning. It was the Wild West in those days; there were no formal training programs. But that left room for folks like me to learn on the job. The rise of e-commerce and web technologies meant I was able to learn many adjacent marketing skills as well. Eventually, I carved out a niche for myself as a marketing technologist, bridging the gap between marketing and IT. In short, I seized the luck and good fortune that landed in my lap and used it to create further opportunities.

Don't get me wrong. For all the privileges I had going for me (white, male, able-bodied, American, etc.), I still ran into numerous roadblocks along the way. It pains me to think of all the disappointment, disgust, and disdain I have encountered over the years. Job interviews, where hiring managers or HR personnel clocked my sexuality. Colleagues who sensed I just wasn't like them. As much personal freedom those of us who cannot pass as straight might reap, there is a terror that comes with the thought of not being able to support yourself by virtue of your sexual orientation, gender orientation, or gender expression. Sitting across from a hiring manager, who is sneering as they wield their authority, is an abhorrent experience. I often look back and wonder what other leaders in these companies would have thought, had they known what was really going on behind closed doors in those interview rooms. But then again, it was their job to know. Those leaders had exactly the company they wanted, otherwise they would have changed it.

GETTING REAL ABOUT CORPORATE BIGOTRY

Companies are just collections of people, and people are imperfect. In some cases, our flaws are just the innocuous expressions of our human design. But in other cases, we have weaponized our shortcomings as a means to make ourselves feel powerful on the backs of others. And many workplaces offer little sanctuary. Sure, nobody wants to think that their choices are born of bigotry. But the reality is if there are not people of all races, genders, and sexual orientations at all levels of our company, then corporate diversity is just lip service. If your company does not explicitly embrace diversity, it does not deserve your talents.

The math is simple: if your boardroom is exclusively a collection of straight, white, cis men, then your company is making racist, sexist, homophobic, and transphobic choices. It does not matter your industry, business category, geography, or the intentions of your mission. There are no excuses. In this day and age, it is incumbent on companies to recognize the intrinsic ethical issues and competitive advantages associated with diversity, and then staff accordingly.

Behind the scenes, here's how this bigotry often works:

- Leaders insist they aren't biased, but when a promotion or opportunity rolls around, they just don't know if you're "ready" or "mature enough" (since only heterosexual, cis men can really display maturity).
- Leaders claim they only hired the best candidate, knowing full well that the interview pool lacked diversity.
- Leaders claim they are not homophobic but deny you opportunities because their clients or customers are

"old school" (a euphemism for their collective bigoted beliefs).

- Leaders tell you how liberal *they* are but fear the *company culture* is awfully conservative (code for you aren't masculine enough, straight enough, etc. for them to risk their career on promoting you).
- Leaders insist you closet yourself (refrain from being less than you are, require you to lie, etc.), just so you can put them at ease.
- Leaders create corporate values (often in the guise of religious freedom) explicitly designed to promote bigotry.

Let's be clear. Bigotry is a form of abuse. It is a way to steal money and power from those who happen to belong to some minority but are equally or more deserving than their peers in the majority. Corporate bigotry is often a form of state-sanctioned theft, since many states in the US deny explicit legal protections for LGBTQIA+ workers. It is welfare for straight, white, cis men, a way to shift capital from one group to another. The impacts are often profound and long-lasting. Those of us denied opportunities are rarely able to recoup any lost money in the long run. In the aggregate, those workers hired instead of us continue to earn raises, bonuses, and promotions at relatively constant rates. Meanwhile, those of us that could not get our foot in the door continue to fall further and further behind, until at the ends of our careers we realize we were never able to catch up.

These impacts are further exacerbated with the increasing geographic segregation of our country. While more and more coastal states and municipalities enact employment legislation protecting LGBTQIA+ workers, many states in the center and south of the country are not yet following suit. That creates a fragmented employment fabric across the country. It falls to workers to advocate for their own best interests, while activists work with legislators to change laws. Not everyone can afford to pick up and move to a state which practices greater equality, but we can all get empowered. We can organize. We can insist on better government representation. We can inform our allies, and we can inform those not yet allied with us. We need not remain victims. If you work for a company that does not value you, it's time to take stock and consider your options.

GETTING REAL ABOUT YOUR PORTABLE EQUITY

Getting empowered starts with being honest about the reality of your situation:

- How much money do you have in savings? What about stocks, mutual funds, 401(k)s or equivalents?
- How long will it take you to find a job of similar compensation?
- Can you realistically cut any expenses in the meantime?
- What sort of pay cut can you afford in a new job, in the name of improving your quality of life? (Remember to consider gaps in healthcare coverage as well.)
- What are the mental, physical, emotional, and spiritual costs of remaining in an abusive employment situation?

These are important questions, but they just represent emergency-level thinking. By the time you start asking yourself these questions, your job, health, or finances might already be in jeopardy. That's why it's important you start a broader assessment before things ever get to this point.

Focus on your portable equity: that compensation you can take with you.

There are four main questions to ask yourself in order to evaluate your portable equity:

- What is the quality and quantity of opportunities available to me in this position? By "opportunities" I specifically mean the chance to do great work, learning, advancement, etc.
- What is the quality and quantity of professional relationships available to me through this position?
- What is my quality and quantity of compensation? Be sure to consider how your compensation is trending, as well as how close you are to any pay ceilings, scheduled raises, etc. Don't forget to include any ancillary compensation, such as Paid Time Off (PTO), vacations, 401(k) matching, etc.
- What is my quality of life at this company? In other words, do I feel valued, respected, part of a team, etc.? Don't forget to consider practical matters, such as the time and distance of your commute, the flexibility of your schedule, etc.

If I can afford to pay my bills and support my family, all things being equal, I keep a keen eye on what I am learning in each opportunity and how it might serve as a lever to lift me to the next opportunity. To a certain degree, I am willing to toil in obscurity if I can continue to solve problems, build value, learn, and grow. Of course, sometimes you just have to turn a buck while you suffer in less-than-ideal situations. However, if you have the resources to sustain you, I encourage you to follow the learnings.

GETTING REAL ABOUT YOUR SALARY

Depending on your field of employment, your salary is often just a part of your total compensation. This can also include various benefits, like healthcare (for which you are only partially charged), contribution matches to retirement accounts (such as a 401(k)), and ancillary goodies (cell phone reimbursement, transit passes, etc.).

In order to find your work/life balance, you need clear goals. But for most of us, our goals are always changing. They change with the seasons of life, accumulated experiences, evolving relationships, and even exigent circumstances. That means evaluating your total compensation as related to your life goals is an important, ongoing meditation:

- Where are you in your life?
- What do you hope to achieve?
- What will it take to get you there?
- Are you in alignment with your core values, mission, and purpose while earning this money?

Your salary alone can be misleading. To consider my quality of pay, I find it useful to calculate my hourly rate: my salary divided by the number of hours I work in a year. I generally assume there are 2,000 work hours in a year (after subtracting PTO), and then add commuting time on top of that. If you are routinely expected to attend office functions and events, make sure to include that time in your calculation as well.

There have been times when I have been given a raise, but my hourly rate actually declined, thanks to all the additional work I absorbed as part of the agreement. In other cases, I have taken jobs at lower pay if it improved my hourly rate, or gave me access to new learnings or opportunities. Just make sure you can afford the hit to your cash flow before you agree to that pay cut. I care so much about my hourly rate, I have long kept my own timesheet to track it. This ensures I maintain a healthy work/life balance, relative to my salary and goals.

Obviously not everybody works full-time, white collar, corporate jobs. Each industry and business sector has different recruiting and human resource standards and best practices. If you don't draw a salary, then you can multiply your hourly wage by the median number of hours you work over the course of a standard month or year. If you do not currently receive any additional compensation, then that should inform your choices and goals.

Ask yourself the following questions:

- Am I looking for a position with a salary or an hourly rate?
- Am I interested in receiving health and retirement benefits, etc.?
- What does it take to win this type of position?
- What do I anticipate the trade-offs might be in accepting such a position?

Your goals are whatever you want them to be, whatever feels right and works for you. The main thing is to make a well-reasoned, mindful choice, so you can feel empowered, and set yourself up for success.

GETTING REAL ABOUT YOUR VALUE

Now that you've landed a job that aligns with your life goals and pays the bills, while also allowing you to contribute to savings, you will likely want to do all you can to keep that job. In order to do that, you've got to learn your value. Without an accurate assessment of your value, you are likely to narrowcast: operate out of scarcity and dream small. Your value is greater than your self-esteem and more than your confidence. Your value is everything that you bring to the table.

For years, I undervalued myself by concentrating primarily on switching costs: how painful and expensive would it be for me to change jobs, and how likely would they be able to match my portable equity? This meant I frequently thought I was overcompensated and underutilized, and when seen through the lens of switching costs, that was often true.

It was not until I learned to evaluate my performance through my employer's eyes that I gained the confidence I needed to take up the space I was due. I was keenly aware of my limits and shortcomings. But by putting myself in the shoes of my boss, I gained clarity on my professional strengths. I realized how much he valued and needed me, how much I helped him, and what his professional life would be like without me.

This exercise gave me a more accurate assessment of my real value. It changed the entire way I engaged with my boss, colleagues, and staff. It gave me the humility and empathy to be curious during times of stress. Granted me the audacity and confidence to express bold opinions to leaders throughout the organization, without being pushy or pretentious. With this new attitude came new recognition. I earned the best reviews of my career and increased my compensation beyond my wildest dreams.

In order to build employer value, you must learn to solve problems. But here's the catch: these problems can't just be little mental exercises that you invent. They have to be actual problems. In other words, you must continuously engage your leaders. Ask them about their professional goals, strategies, and tactics. Inquire about their pain points. And then listen. I mean really listen. Not just to the words they say, but to the words they don't say. Watch the expressions on their faces and hear their tones of voice. Empathize with them, both verbally and attitudinally.

Whatever your industry or field, no matter your rank or role, just about everyone has a boss. Perhaps your boss is a board of directors, a group of investors, or a business partner. Or maybe you're in a more traditional role and report directly to a manager. Whatever the case, you will be well-served to proactively engage your boss. Continue to gingerly extract the information you need, so you can effectively help them reach their goals and solve their problems. Then match these issues to your superpowers, those skills of yours that are rare, if not inimitable. These skills are your differentiator, both from other job applicants and other coworkers. When well-honed, they become your competitive advantage. In fact, if you are successful at accomplishing just this, you will likely have a job as long as you want.

GETTING REAL ABOUT CONTINUING EDUCATION

Continuing education is a life and career requirement for all of us. No matter our industry or field of study, it is imperative that we all learn and grow over the course of our entire career. It is the single best way to stay engaged and feel empowered. There are any number of ways (both in person and online) to learn more about your subject matter, adjacent topics, or business in general. Here are a few to get you started:

- Degree programs
- Certificate programs
- Independent classes
- Public speaking events with subject matter experts
- Conferences
- Webinars
- Books

Most of us will utilize a variety of these educational opportunities over the course of our career. Not only can they be powerful tools to increase your knowledge and build your credentials, but they can also be wonderful ways to increase the quantity and quality of your professional network. There is an overabundance of information available to all of us. So how in the heck are we supposed to evaluate all these options? This challenge is magnified when considering the associated costs (time, energy, tuition, travel, accommodations, etc.). Like most things, I recommend a combination of intuition, advice from mentors and colleagues, and sanity checks with your loved ones. Do your research and talk to those you trust.

In 2012 (at the age of thirty-seven), I decided to go back to school. My undergraduate and graduate degrees were in music performance, which ranked surprisingly low on the desired list of attributes corporate recruiters considered when searching for potential job applicants in my field. With the rise of Big Data, I realized these recruiters were doing keyword searches on résumés and social media profiles. In my field, a Master of Business Administration (MBA) is at the top of the list of requirements, especially when considering my other degrees. Without that piece of paper, I assumed recruiters and hiring managers would discount any future applications for positions above my current level.

Even though I love to learn, going back to school was about the last thing I wanted to do. I had a stressful job and a full life outside of work. But I was the breadwinner in my family and knew I needed to increase my earning potential. And then fate intervened. My company created a scholarship to pay the tuition at our local state university for the perfect program: an Executive MBA program meant for full-time professionals. So I knew I had to throw my hat in the ring.

I was selected as one of the winners of this scholarship and began the MBA program. Over the next two years, I worked harder than I ever thought possible. I was simply unqualified to compete in a program like this. It was a real lesson. In retrospect, I probably should have entered a less rigorous program, comprised of students with more nontraditional backgrounds, like myself. But at the end of the day, I learned a tremendous amount of information and came away with all sorts of great professional relationships that I could leverage in any number of ways. But make no bones about it: the cost was high.

You do not have to be good at everything. That's impossible.

The key is to know your strengths and find creative ways to leverage them. Take a long, hard look at your weaknesses. In some cases, you will decide to shore those up with additional education, training, or experience. But sometimes, you will make the pragmatic choice to live with your weaknesses and surround yourself with people whose strengths correspond to them. That way you will complement each other. When missions and incentives also align, these complementary relationships can be highly effective. They form the basis of teamwork, which is essential in helping a business thrive.

GETTING REAL ABOUT YOUR PROFESSIONAL STORY

As you accelerate your career, it is imperative you continuously improve the ways you tell your professional story. This goes beyond your résumé. Your résumé should be up to date, but most hiring managers will just glance at it anyway. Far more important is your ability to convincingly and passionately summarize your work experience over the phone, on video, and in person. You cannot practice this too much, especially since your professional story will always be changing. Depending on your field, this might also require supplemental materials, such as an online portfolio or video reel.

Before you walk into a meeting, you should be able to confidently address these issues with any potential partner, employer, investor, etc.:

- What value did you build at your company?
- How do you quantify and qualify that value?

- How did your value help the company's bottom line? (Hint: you must thoroughly understand your company's business model and be able to succinctly articulate your role in it.)
- Specifically, why were you successful at your company?

I would never hire anybody who cannot clearly explain their employer's business model, regardless of their position, role, or industry. All workers contribute to the bottom line. If they are not at least broadly aware of the underlying mechanics of their company's revenue generation, go-to-market strategy, and customer base, why would I assume they would ever learn it at a new company? Most companies do not make this information readily available; you must be prepared to chase it down. Approach this task like a journalist and delicately extract the information from those in your company whom you trust.

Perfecting your professional story will also help you take charge of your professional reputation. Your reputation refers to how others describe you when you are not in the room. Reputations are strange and elusive because they reside exclusively in the minds of others. People are often easily influenced and highly irrational. That's why reputations are so easily undone and must be so painstakingly rebuilt. The key is to focus on the energy you bring to every situation. How do people feel when you enter the room? How about when you leave?

Before each interaction, take a moment to breathe and center yourself. Consider your desired outcome, as well as any likely obstacles or concerns. And then remember this: in most situations, your professional relationships are far more valuable (both to you and the company) than your actual work product. It took years for me to accept and internalize this. As an introvert and an idealist, I wanted my work to speak for itself. But it doesn't. I have to tell the story. To people. Over and over. And when I'm able to find the joy in that, I raise the energy levels of everyone around me. And that's what gives me a reputation of which I can be proud.

GETTING REAL ABOUT JOB APPLICATIONS

It's no secret that we're all drowning in data. Hiring managers and recruiters are no different. They are often forced to sift through hundreds of résumés for each open position, and 90 percent of these candidates are often completely unqualified. The thing about the ease of the internet is that it means anyone can apply for any job, regardless of their qualifications. For some job candidates, fear gets the better of them. They can't seem to help themselves and apply to every job they see.

Not to be outdone, the hiring managers and recruiters have turned to applicant tracking systems to help them manage all this information. They use these computer applications to home in on specific keywords and do all the initial qualification searching. But there has been a huge downside to this battle: qualified applicants invariably get lost in the shuffle. If their cover letters or résumés do not happen to have the precise combination of acronyms or keywords sought by the applicant tracking system, they will likely never even get an interview. This leaves everyone feeling frustrated.

Of course, all of this assumes you are submitting your materials as part of the old cattle call. As always, the best way to apply for any position is to leverage your professional relationships. It's far better to have one of your contacts, who happens to work for your desired company, drop your résumé directly on the hiring manager's desk, than to submit it blindly. Better still for them to accompany your application with a conversation. In fact, many jobs are never even advertised, because hiring managers desperately fear being inundated with unqualified candidates. In their eyes, truly qualified candidates are tough to find. And even qualified candidates sometimes exaggerate their work history, skills, or experience. Hiring managers often think it's far safer just to hire someone they already know and trust. Even if they are sub-optimizing on skills, they are able to control for character, which for them makes it worth the risk.

Applying for jobs is just about the most draining activity on the planet, so cut yourself some slack and realize you are not alone. Just about everybody hates it. And to make matters worse, once you submit your application, the truly grueling part begins: the waiting game. It's a known fact that every second that follows your pressing of the submit button on your targeted company's career site feels like an eternity. So stop, breathe, and look at things from the hiring manager's perspective.

Hiring managers are busy. Just about the last thing they want to do is read résumés, but they know they must. And they will, but in most cases, it's just going to take them awhile. They too often forget that there's a real person on the other end of that résumé. And days go by. Then days turn into weeks, and weeks sometimes turn into months. Seriously. I'm just trying to explain it, not excuse it. So as an applicant, please don't take it personally. And please don't panic and apply for jobs for which you are unqualified. That's only going to feel disempowering in the long run. Practice confidence, dignity, and patience. And after a certain amount of time has elapsed, feel free to check on the status of your application. But do so carefully and with a light touch. After you have initially sought further information, that's it. You're done. If you don't hear back, it's time to move on. There are greener pastures out there. If the staff at that company cannot respond to your simple email inquiry, then I doubt you would want to work there anyway.

By the time you receive an offer for an initial interview, most hiring managers have already determined that your résumé qualifies you for the work. From here on out they are trying to evaluate how well you will fit on their team and in their company culture. Every team and every company has a culture. Sometimes they work in concert, while in other cases they conflict. And all things being equal, culture always wins. That's why smart hiring managers assess minimum technical requirements first, followed by character and culture, and then return to advanced technical requirements at the end of the evaluation. It's also why they are likely to have you meet a wide range of employees during the interview process—they often think they are more likely to get your future colleagues excited about your candidacy if they meet you in person.

In corporate settings, the arc of the job interview often looks something like this.

Pre-Screen: A corporate recruiter will talk to you via email and over the phone to assess basic character qualities and aptitudes; punctuality, verbal and written skills, professional demeanor, background, professional goals, basic skills matching, etc. In most cases, recruiters do not have the subject matter expertise to conduct a full skills-matching assessment, so this is just a smoke test. They just want to get you talking. At the end of the interview, they will also assess your compensation expectations and might inquire as to your current or previous compensation levels. So be prepared with a strategy in mind to discuss this topic, or sidestep it altogether. Don't just try to wing it.

Phone Interview: If you pass the pre-screen, the recruiter will use their applicant tracking system to submit your résumé to the pertinent hiring manager. For candidates they really like, recruiters might follow that up with an email, phone call, or an in-person conversation with the hiring manager. Most recruiters are paid on commission and have a vested financial incentive in advocating for applicants they deem highly qualified or easily placed. Depending on how the hiring manager feels about your application, you will get invited by the recruiter for a phone interview. Otherwise you might never hear from this company, or perhaps just get some sort of communication in several weeks (or even months) stating that you've been ruled out entirely. The phone interview itself is likely to last between fifteen and thirty minutes. At this stage, the hiring manager is assessing your likeability and overall storytelling ability. Can you clearly, concisely, and cogently repeat highlights from your résumé and cover letter? Do you have smart questions regarding the position or company at hand, which demonstrate you have done some initial research?

First Interview: This is where things differ the most from company to company. Most often, you will only meet with the hiring manager. They want to validate their choice to engage with you before taking up valuable time with their staff or putting their reputations on the line. At this stage (just like in the pre-screen), they are assessing basic character qualities and aptitudes: promptness, professional demeanor, professional attire, etc. But now the single biggest test is likeability. It's challenging to forge a relationship exclusively over the phone. Now that you are meeting in person, they can start to get a true sense of you. Be careful: You are being evaluated every second you are in the building. Everyone from the receptionist to the office manager to the recruiter is likely to swing by and pass judgment. This is very much a performance, and you're the one on stage.

You will likely get further probing questions into your skills and expertise, but in many cases, these will still be at a relatively high level. Many hiring managers are no longer daily contributors in their areas of expertise, so leave the true technical evaluation up to their staff. Your first interview is likely to last an hour, at the end of which you will typically have no indication of how you performed and be forced to once again play the waiting game. If the hiring manager really likes you and fears you might be interviewing with other companies (especially competitors), they might tip their hand a bit to try and charm you. But often you will leave without having a clue.

Second Interview: In many cases, this is where you first meet the staff. Depending on the size of the team, this interview can literally last all day. But that's pretty rare. It's often two hours of intense questions on a variety of topics, from a variety of subject matter experts throughout the company.

They want to accept and embrace you, but only if they can make you suffer a little in the process. Look at it from their perspective: the last thing they want is to give their professional stamp of approval to someone who turns out to be unqualified or a pain in the neck. So while you will definitely be evaluated on culture, most of their scrutiny will be reserved for your technical aptitude. Depending on the nature of the job, you can expect to be asked to solve problems on the fly or to present any "homework" which the hiring manager requested of you in the first interview. Make sure you interview them too. I assure you they will have nothing but respect for articulate, well-reasoned questions. In fact, asking no questions is a huge red flag. The staff is rarely going to give you any indication at all of your performance, since they won't want to upstage the hiring manager. But at the end of the session, the hiring manager is likely to pop back in and chat with you a bit. They will have already discussed your performance privately with each team member you met and will be well-informed of their thoughts and opinions prior to this closing session with you. Depending on how highly they think of you, this session will feel a lot like some strange form of corporate flirting. And that's okay. It's all part of the dance.

Final Interview: Often the hiring manager does not have unilateral authority to make a final decision. They might be required to consult with their peers or even their supervisor, and often this means that you must meet an additional group of people. Since meeting all these people can cost the company lots of time and money, this round is often reserved for senior positions or positions in smaller companies.

At this stage of the process, the hiring manager is your best friend. You can be sure they are actively advocating for you to either be hired or to be part of a very short list. There is no way they are going to stick their neck out and recommend you to their peers or senior leaders unless they feel great about your application. Because the people in this round often have no direct practitioner experience in your area of expertise, the questions are likely to be fairly broad. But don't let that fool you. These are likely very smart people with finely honed antennae. You must paint a vivid and compelling story of what brought you to this point in your career and why they should take a chance on you. You will need a polished and professional response to any gaps in time, rank, or expertise on your résumé. You will likely spend thirty minutes with each person you meet in this round.

At the end of this session, it's once again time for the waiting game. Executives often love to drag their feet with hiring decisions. Since they are not bearing the burden of an increased workload while headcount goes unfilled, there is often little incentive for them to pull the trigger and bless the final hire. This dilemma is compounded when you factor the considerable time and expense it takes in many cases to fire an employee. That means often the executive and the hiring manager that reports to them will end up in a game of cat and mouse, while you are left on the sidelines wringing your hands.

Negotiations: Good recruiters will talk pay early and often. They will try to close the hiring managers high when opening the initial job requisition, and then close candidates low during the interview process. Not only does this strategy give the recruiters wiggle room, but it can also give them leverage, particularly when considering their commission-based compensation structure. If for some reason the recruiter or hiring manager does not initiate a conversation about pay, I highly encourage you to take the lead. You are doing nobody any favors to avoid the topic, and you will waste everyone's time if your expectations are dramatically different than what they can offer.

There is currently a great debate in the corporate world about compensation strategies. However, most companies still set salaries at some mystical combination of what the market will bear (in other words, what similar positions are going for) and what did/do you as a candidate make at your previous/current position. In many respects, this approach is just silly, but it is likely the one you will encounter. Now is the time to negotiate. If you miss this window, you will not likely get another opportunity until your annual review, or you personally raise the issue in some way.

Other people are negotiating pay with each job they take. If you chicken out, then you will fall further and further behind everyone else. You will simply never make up that missed pay over the course of your career. Now is the time—do it. There are other items you should negotiate as part of this process, including your start date, vacation schedule, and PTO. Everything is negotiable. Everything. But negotiation is an art. You have to know your value and accurately assess you leverage (or lack thereof), and then effectively use that information to force a confrontation. That means you might need to be ready to walk away from an opportunity altogether.

Offer Letter: In many cases, when everything has gone

well, the recruiter will call you to make the actual offer. The reason they do this is to finalize negotiations, from an HR perspective, and also to remove this workload from the hiring manager. They typically prefer to call you on the phone because there will be no written record of the conversation. So I recommend you record it. But be careful; in the US, laws around recording these calls differ by state, so make sure you check those first.

Not only will your recording be a handy reference document once your adrenaline fades and you forget the terms of your offer, but it also becomes an artifact to help you navigate through any potential dispute resolution. If the call goes well, the recruiter will send you an offer letter. Depending on the organization, this might arrive via email or snail mail. Make sure you read this letter carefully prior to responding. Once you accept the offer, changing the terms will be very difficult. Your temptation will be to rush through this part of the process out of excitement. Don't. Stop, breathe, and take your time. Then when you're ready, move forward on your terms. You have all the power at this point. It may be the last time in your relationship with this company that you hold this much power, so use it wisely and well.

Obviously, not every application process will be the same or follow this flow exactly. Every company is different. Every hiring manager is different. But hopefully this outline gives you a sense of what you might expect, so you can enter this process feeling more informed and empowered.

GETTING REAL ABOUT SIDE HUSTLES

Sometimes one job is just not enough to pay the bills. Or

even if it is, maybe your goals require additional capital. These situations leave you with a handful of choices, one of which might be taking on additional work. Depending on the specifics of your situation, this additional work could take the form of consulting, a part-time job, or something more entrepreneurial. If you go down this road, the key is that you continue to take care of the job that sustains you. Reduced performance levels at your primary place of employment are simply not an option. It does you no good to give what you don't have and reach beyond your capacity. You must be exceptionally careful and wade into this process slowly.

As you evaluate this opportunity, consider the following:

- How much money will you really be adding to your savings, after taxes and additional costs, such as gas, travel, uniform/clothes, etc.?
- How much will this opportunity drain your energy? You might not be able to afford the additional toll on your mind, body, and spirit. Or it might not be worth it, relative to your additional anticipated revenue.
- Do you have an escape plan if it all goes to hell? What will that escape plan cost you, in terms of time, energy, and relationships impacted?
- How will you measure your success in this new work? When you're in the thick of things, it can be tough to know how well or how poorly it's going. Do you have trusted, objective resources who will give you their candid feedback? Are there any other objective metrics you can use, such as monitoring your actual contributions towards savings, calculating your new adjusted hourly rate, calculating your total hours worked, etc.?

What I have found is that every extra dollar I make costs me something in return; sometimes taking on additional work can have unintended consequences. I encourage you to be careful about jumping into anything that might be tough to unravel. Consider your opportunity from all angles. Discuss it with those you love, trust, and respect. Make sure you are crystal clear with your loved ones about the costs they will bear, such as less time with you, more stress in your relationships due to your reduced capacity, etc. Then give yourself permission to bail if it all gets overwhelming. The last thing you want to do is put yourself in a situation where you feel trapped. You will need an exit strategy that allows all those involved to save face and minimize any negative impacts.

SUMMARY

Look, it's no secret that life isn't fair. And those of us burdened with being part of some minority know this better than most. But at the end of the day, we are each of us responsible for our attitude, work ethic, discipline, determination, and passion. Most of us will eventually get a shot, provided we show up with an abundance of energy and enthusiasm. If we complement that with thoughtful research, we will be positioned to plow through many obstacles and seize any opportunities that arise.

But in order for that to happen, you must be prepared. You need a clear understanding of who you are and what you want. What are your strengths? Weaknesses? What are your goals in terms of work/life balance, professional goals, quality of pay, etc.? Do you require any credentials, certificates, degrees, etc. to land that dream job? If so, what are the costs to achieve those? If you are looking for a new job, do you have a targeted company or a short list of companies in mind? If so, is there anybody in your professional network who can introduce you to the hiring manager or recruiter, or at least submit your application on your behalf? Or do you need to invest in the growth of your professional network in order to prepare for a future opportunity or job search? Are you ready to run the gauntlet of the job interview process? Have you done your research and prepared your materials?

When it comes to managing your career, you can expect the unexpected. But this is what's so exciting! Your career might ebb and flow, or change course altogether, but outside of extreme circumstances, your career will span the whole of your adult life. All the more reason to take charge now, so you can steer the ship where you want it to go.

CHAPTER 5

FINANCES

I was born into a middle-class family that knew nothing about money, or at least nothing they were willing to teach me. Some in my family lived with chronic indebtedness—born of addiction, financial mismanagement, or self-sabotage. Generation after generation racing to the bottom. Others in my family somehow flourished financially, leading ostensibly "normal" suburban lives. Why some in my family were haves and others were have-nots, was all a great mystery. Those that had money still had plenty of issues, so why did their financial health not seem to be one of them?

I grew up believing in the lottery of life. Some of us would just never make it rich without divine intervention. This was just another way of saying that I believed there was nothing I could do to lift myself out of my circumstances, unless I got lucky. I was mired in self-pity, and felt completely disempowered. I had a vision of wealth born out of scarcity and envy, a poverty of the mind. I knew nothing about creating or maintaining a sustainable income and was wholly unprepared for adulthood.

Society reinforced my ignorance by perpetuating myths about gay men that involved ostracism, AIDS, and irresponsibility—making it clear that it was pointless for us to plan for a future that would never come. Gay men were doomed to die miserable and alone. There was no hope of seeing our thirties, much less our retirement, so what use did we have for a 401(k)? Why should we bother to start businesses, when straight people would not dare buy products from such pariahs? We were less living for the moment than living as if there were no tomorrow.

Many straight children are given a leg up in life. Parents help pay for initial mortgages, often as part of a wedding gift. They tuck tidy sums of money into their children's checking accounts, just because. Or they groom their children for corporate positions, through patrimony and influence. Recently, this spoils system has been changing somewhat, but don't let anyone ever tell you that there is no American aristocracy. Little princes and princesses are still trained to inherit the world so they might perpetuate it for future generations. Happy, straight, white, cis men and women, wrapped in a bubble of privilege and denial—floating on, forever and ever, amen.

Too many gay men on the other hand are kicked out of their homes, left to fend for themselves, and forced to carve a cleft in the rock of the world that they might climb into. Others are shunted to the corners of their family tree—ignored, or ridiculed, but certainly not invested in. For me, it became clear that there would be no safety nets or guardrails. Everything I would earn I would have to earn myself, with my own two hands. Hustling, driving, and pushing forward relentlessly. And that's okay. I'm in good company. There are so many of us, of all genders, races, abilities, and sexual orientations, who were denied advantages. Somehow we endure, and sometimes we even prosper.

If you are a gay man wondering how in the hell you will ever catch up to your straight peers of privilege, take heart. This chapter is for you, to give you the beginning of an education in a topic that is your birthright. Perhaps this education was stolen from you, through the bigoted beliefs of your family, or a society that would rather not think too much about whom it banishes. There is a wealth of information out there at your fingertips, ready for the taking, and much of it free. All you must do is acknowledge the reality of your situation, set aside your grief and your rage, and then lift yourself up.

GETTING REAL ABOUT WEALTH AND FINANCIAL INDEPENDENCE

We are all born into this world in different circumstances. Some of us have parents who struggle to make ends meet. Others have families who have built wealth for generations. But the truth is, all of us can learn to be a little more financially independent, no matter our mix of privilege and adversity. The road to financial freedom starts with our beliefs. When most of us think of "wealth," we think of amassing large sums of cash. But wealth is much broader than money. It implies choice and opportunity. Money is just a means to an end, and to hoard cash in a world of inequality is to walk through a moral minefield.

We achieve financial independence only when the cash flow from our investments exceeds our expenses. This independence can last a moment or a lifetime, depending on how we play our cards. It has nothing to do with how many assets we accumulate. Cash is what we spend, which means cash is what we require. Our assets are just a means to earn more cash. It's really quite simple, but that doesn't make it easy. It requires vision, self-awareness, discipline, and hustle. Financial independence is not a goal for everyone. We all have different values, wants, and needs. The amount of money we have in the bank has nothing to do with our intrinsic value.

We can be "wealthy" long before we achieve financial independence. To be wealthy, we need just enough money to sustain our quality of life, and to afford those choices and opportunities we hold dear. We might still need to work a full-time job in order to fund that life. Some of us might even require a full-time job with a side hustle. That's how being wealthy is different from financial independence. For example, you don't have to be financially independent to start your own business. You just need enough money to cover your fixed costs and contribute to your variable costs, while maintaining your prudent reserve.

Wealth implies a certain price insensitivity. That means we can make choices based on value, rather than price, and money is no longer a primary obstacle to our lifestyle. A wealthy life is based on relationships and experiences, rather than the accumulation of things. The pursuit of objects for their own sake is one of the major pitfalls many experience on their path to financial independence. At a certain point, happiness is not tied to money. If we can pay our bills and feed our families, making more money often comes with diminishing returns. That means the effort we expend to earn extra money yields less and less happiness. It's not that more money makes you unhappy. It's just that once your core expenses are covered, this extra money is unlikely to enhance your daily life. But even more importantly, the only way to keep something is to give it away. Ultimately, generosity is the true source of fulfillment.

Some of us seek financial independence through the latest stock tip, but trying to predict the future is a fool's errand. Others try to back their way into financial independence through extreme frugality, relentlessly optimizing their lives based on minimizing their expenses. The old adage is the simplest advice: spend less, save more, and invest the difference wisely. This approach is based on savings as a percentage of income and the rate of return on your investments relative to inflation. But what most of us don't consider is the inevitable boundaries it presents. We can only pare down our expenses so much. Often others are impacted along the way: spouses, children, family, friends, etc. So this approach is not viable after a certain point. And at the end of the day, most of us start to wonder about all the experiences we might be missing, especially if we are young. Once youth passes us by, it's gone forever. Money may come and go, but time constantly slips through our fingers. The extreme frugality and asceticism required by most to generate the necessary finances for investment can seem onerous. Fortunately, there are other ways to crack this nut.

If you are fortunate enough to have an income that allows you to squirrel away money while paring back just a little on expenses, then you will generate a savings faster than you might otherwise imagine. For most of us, this savings becomes our initial prudent reserve (six to twelve months of anticipated expenses, depending on the details of our situation). Sometimes life just requires a few thousand dollars from us out of the blue, so I recommend keeping your prudent reserve relatively liquid. In this case, it's probably best kept in a savings account. The value in this approach is in the liquidity of the investment, meaning you can draw from it in a moment's notice, with no fees. If you have yet to establish a prudent reserve, it likely means you are living from paycheck to paycheck. You've got a lot of work to do, and this is job one. You might need to revisit chapter six in this book ("Career"), in order to reassess your career or compensation options, such that you have enough cash to invest in yourself first.

GETTING REAL ABOUT INVESTING

After you have established a stable prudent reserve, it's time to start planning an investment strategy that works for you. We are all different. We have different wants, needs, and risk tolerances. The key is to know yourself. If you're part of a family, it is critical you communicate clearly with everyone, so you can find an approach that works for all of you. This will likely involve compromise, but healthy communication now will save you headaches down the line. As part of this conversation, I recommend you focus on both the risks and the rewards.

Ask yourself (and your family) these questions:

- How much money do I need in my savings account in order to *feel* safe? Does this amount differ from what my family needs?

- How much longer do I want to work? What about my family?
- How much longer do I realistically think I can work (based on my anticipated mental and physical well-being)? What about my family?
- How much unsecured debt (typically, credit cards) do I currently hold? What about my family? And what is our repayment plan?
- How much secured debt (typically refers to mortgage, car payment, etc.) do I hold? What about my family? And what is our repayment plan?
- What is our source of wealth? Is it stable and predictable?

Based on your answers to these questions, you can formulate an investing approach that everyone in your household can celebrate. Built into these questions is the assumption that you can quantify your income and expenses, and then monitor those over time. If you have a simple financial portfolio, you might just use a spreadsheet to track this information. However, if your financial portfolio is more complex, there are numerous software applications to help you do this. The main thing is that you track your income and expenses reliably and consistently over time.

Implicit in these questions is the assumption that you pay down all your unsecured debt as quickly as possible, since it typically carries high interest rates. If you are not yet well on your way to eliminating your unsecured debt, it is crucial you do this as soon as you have established a prudent reserve. In fact, paying down this debt is so important, you might allow your prudent reserve to run lower than normal for a brief time. It all depends on the balance of your savings to your debt. In extreme cases, paying down this debt may not be an option. In those situations, I advise you work quickly to either restructure your debt, seek outside assistance, or file for bankruptcy protection. Do not slip into a denial now that will reduce your opportunities in the long run.

Investments are commodities, which means anybody can buy them. But the returns will vary. The difference is you. You are your own most valuable asset, so pay yourself first. Defer a certain percentage of your income before it hits each paycheck with investment accounts like 401(k) s and Health Savings Accounts (HSAs). Then siphon off a predictable percentage of your paycheck each month into a standard savings account. The key here is not the interest you will earn, but the pride you will develop in watching the balance in these accounts grow over time. Next, pay off all your unsecured debt and plan for any upcoming known expenses, whether they are regularly recurring expenses or one-offs. Any money left over is yours to invest.

When it comes to investing, there are several categories to consider:

- Paper (stocks and bonds)
- Business Entrepreneurship (direct ownership of a company)
- Real Estate (direct ownership of property)

Not everyone needs to invest in all three categories. For many, that will just be too complicated to sustain, especially with your long term, active participation. Most of us will choose to invest in two out of three of these categories—typically paper combined with either business entrepreneurship or real estate.

For instance, I have an aversion to real estate, but an affinity for business entrepreneurship. I can barely take care of my own house, much less run a multi-family dwelling. I'm also deeply skeptical of (bordering on moral opposition to) the stock market. I limit my investments to low-level income deferrals, such as a 401(k) and an HSA. On the other hand, I have an MBA and love to solve business problems. I am also self-reliant, resilient, and smart. Yet I have a relatively small support network and live with a variety of mental health challenges. Taking all of this into account, it is clear I have a passion for business entrepreneurship, which I fund with my traditional career (in digital marketing) and meager paper assets. The point is you have to know yourself and then make realistic choices that are right for you.

GETTING REAL ABOUT FINANCIAL PLANNING

Most financial planners will start any consultation by asking you basic questions about your income and expenses. They then put this information into a software application that magically creates a list of recommended low-cost, passive index funds, using a traditional asset allocation. While this approach is certainly viable, there are several components of which you should be aware prior to purchasing anything in this category.

I have a bias towards action. I want to be involved. I want to understand where I'm putting my money. So I hate the idea of just handing a check over to someone, crossing my fingers, and hoping for the best. When money is involved,

I always want to understand the incentives of the various players. If you have a financial planner, you might think about asking them how they make their money. If their income is somehow influencing their investment advice, you might want to understand precisely how. As you start working with a financial planner, most will ask you all sorts of questions to which you will not have the answer. Things like "How long do you expect to live?" and "What will be the rate of inflation at your retirement?" Your answers to these questions are not trivial where the underlying math is concerned. Since there is no way you can know the answers, it means your financial planner's calculations, and their subsequent advice, will be based on a chain of assumptions.

It's one thing for an insurance company to use actuarial tables to calculate aggregate customer life expectancy, but when it comes to your personal financial planning, your information is particular to you. Due to the way the underlying math works, guesswork just isn't good enough. The key numbers in traditional retirement planning are savings as a percentage of income, and return on investment minus inflation. But if you don't know when you will retire, how long you will live, or the inflation levels at the time of divestment, your predictions will likely be wildly inaccurate.

This approach is about developing a model of your financial planning in preparation for retirement. But models are intrinsically wrong. If you are determined to work with a financial model, I recommend altering the underlying assumptions based on various criteria. That way, you can at least stress test the results, in order to determine a confidence interval. Over time, this should paint a picture that ends up being a little closer to reality. Your model will still be wrong, but not *as* wrong.

There are two different equations that determine your wealth growth:

1. The mathematical expectancy equation: (Probability of win * Average win) – (Probability of loss * Average loss)
2. The future value equation: (Present Value * (1 + the rate of return)^# of years)

Put into words, the mathematical expectancy equation determines the compound growth rate of your assets: how much you make when you're right, minus how much you lose when you're wrong, multiplied by how frequently you're either right or wrong. The future value equation is a method to determine the future value of money, in order to help you adjust your expectations for inflation. In other words, it attempts to predict how much your assets will grow and by what date.

Don't worry! If you dislike math, there are tons of free calculators out there to help you with these equations. The larger issue is the underlying assumptions. It's imperative you understand that the values which these equations determine will be inaccurate; you must come at the data from a variety of angles in order to improve your model. Most of us will require professional help to do this, so hire an expert.

GETTING REAL ABOUT RETIREMENT PLANNING

Retirement ain't what it used to be—at least for a growing number of Americans, who are staying healthy and living longer. On the one hand, that means they will have to generate more income, in order to fund their longevity. But on the other hand, they will have more time and energy with which to do it. For many of us, the appeal of playing golf all day and standing in cruise ship buffet lines has lost its luster. Instead, we are opting to preserve our vitality and professional relevance by shifting, or even changing, our careers.

The new retirement looks something like this:

- Get your basic financial house in order.
- Accumulate a certain amount of diversified core assets that will generate cash in the background.
- Downshift your career to focus on service and personal fulfillment.
- Earn just enough to cover your reduced fixed costs, while making a contribution to your variable costs.
- Use the assets generating cash in the background to pay remaining variable costs and contribute to savings, as you prepare for the day that you finally and permanently age out of the workforce.

So how much money do you need to retire, anyway? The answer is nobody knows because nobody can predict the future. If you need a magic number to feel more confident about your financial planning, there are various rules of thumb. For instance, "The Rule of 300" states that every $1k you plan to spend in your retirement requires 300 times that in assets to support. On the other hand, the "4% Rule" states that a retiree can withdraw 4 percent of their investments in the first year of retirement, and in subsequent years increase that amount by the rate of inflation. But these rules are just loose, one-size-fits-all guidelines to help you sanity check your plan and feel more confident. In no way should you use them to bypass the hard work of active financial planning with a paid professional.

As we discussed earlier, it's all about managing risk and expectancy. It turns out there is science here, not just art. Mathematical expectancy is a way to develop statistical confidence about an inherently unknowable future. Expectancy is different than probability. Probability describes the likelihood of an event. Expectancy extends that description to also include the payoff when that event occurs. For example, if you flip a coin, there is a 50 percent probability that it will land on heads. But that statement describes nothing about the associated payoff. What if I pay you ten dollars each time the coin lands on heads? Or, what if I pay you five dollars each time it lands on heads, and *you* pay *me* ten dollars each time it lands on tails? That's expectancy. It's not important that you can solve these equations; you can pay people to help you with that. The main point is that you understand how the payoff changes the math.

Everybody likes to be right, and we would all love to be able to predict the future. Let it go. You are wrong about many things every day of your life. You will never be able to predict the future. Instead, focus on risk management. If you manage risk well, you can be wrong the vast majority of the time and still build wealth. Most people hesitate to get in the game, because they fear their capacity. They just don't think they have the knowledge, education, or aptitude to juggle all of these concepts. They let their fears get the better of them and assume they will mess it all up. And they will! What they misunderstand is that the underlying math means they *can* mess it up and *still* build wealth, as long as they learn to manage risk.

GETTING REAL ABOUT LEVERAGE

Leverage is any tool that allows you to expand your resources beyond your limitations, in order to produce greater results than you alone could generate. When applied correctly, it helps you multiply reward without increasing risk. You simply cannot build wealth without leverage. In our jobs, we leverage time for money. But the vast majority of us will never land a job that pays an hourly rate capable of building true wealth. There just aren't enough hours in the day! When most people think of leverage, they think of financial leverage and cringe, since it increases both risk and return. But there are many types of leverage:

- **Financial Leverage:** leveraging other people's money removes the constraint of what's in your wallet.
- **Time Leverage:** leveraging other people's time removes the constraint of your twenty-four hours in any given day.
- **Technology Leverage:** leveraging systems and applications helps you work more efficiently and effectively.
- **Marketing Leverage:** leveraging media to extend your audience reach removes the constraint of one-on-one communication.
- **Social Leverage:** leveraging other people's networks and connections extends your reach to both more people and more *types* of people.
- **Knowledge Leverage:** leveraging the talents, expertise, experience, aptitudes, and affinities of others extends what you alone happen to know, to what others know and have experienced.

Leverage allows you to build more wealth than you alone could ever hope to achieve. It allows you to extend your reach and resources beyond your personal limitations. It can also be mutually beneficial: it creates wealth, builds community, and offers people the chance to learn and grow. Leverage not only builds wealth faster (by separating wealth growth from return on equity constraints), but it also removes obstacles. Leverage unlocks the full potential of the larger community, allowing you to work asymmetrically to achieve geometric gains. If you are not effectively utilizing leverage, you are working too hard, only to be running in place. Stop. Breathe. Think. Utilize. Delegate. Trust. Verify. This is how you will get ahead.

GETTING REAL ABOUT PAPER ASSETS

Paper assets offer a path to financial independence in ten to fifteen years, without restructuring your job or enhancing your income. But they only work if you dramatically cut costs. Investing inevitably involves risking capital on an unknowable future. The key word is "risk," and risk management must come first. It's critical that you understand the pros and cons of this investment category before jumping in. The underlying math means that you need to be prepared for periodic drawdowns of up to 45 percent. In the past, these drawdowns have lasted for years. Recently they have been brief, so while they might have been news-making events, their impact on everyone's portfolio has been somewhat limited. It's the sustained drawdowns that should worry you. And remember, extreme volatility is not limited to equities. Stocks and bonds can correlate to the downside. Equities and bonds both perform worse during periods of inflation. Inflation is a problem during inflationary recessions because, in these environments, the Federal Reserve lacks the ability to bail out investors by lowering interest rates.

The math here is based on asymmetrically compounding gains and losses. For instance, if you start with a $100 investment and you lose 10 percent, you actually have to make 11.1 percent to return to even. A 10 percent loss requires an 11.1 percent gain to return to even, which is what makes it asymmetric. But wait, it gets worse. A 25 percent loss requires a 33 percent gain to return to even, and a 50 percent loss requires a 100 percent gain to return to even. But the math gets *even worse*. These examples are just depicting theoretical mathematical relationships. In the real world, it might take even longer for your portfolio to recover, thanks to inflation, transaction fees, or unanticipated expenses. That is a harsh reality all of us should consider before putting any money into this investment category.

But the good news is that over a long-time horizon, this investment category will definitely pay off. It just won't make you rich quickly. Think about it: have you ever heard of a twenty-something millionaire who got rich by investing in mutual funds? Of course not. Paper assets are great for the long haul, provided you can weather the storms along the way. But this category is not a get-rich-quick scheme.

Everybody wants to know how they can pick the next hot investment. The truth is you can't. Anybody who tells you otherwise is being dishonest. It's far better to create an investing approach that works for you, by generating a mathematically viable positive growth expectancy over the long term. Trying to buy stock in some company that you hope will be the next Apple or Google is a fool's errand, and jumping on hot tips from friends is a quick way to lose both your money and your friends. Go slow. Stick to what works. Keep your eyes on your own paper. Be true to yourself. Get engaged and take ownership. Be patient. The rewards will come.

GETTING REAL ABOUT BUSINESS ENTREPRENEURSHIP

Business entrepreneurship is an investment category governed by entirely different math than paper investments. It does not compound from the equity side of the equation because, instead of leveraging money, it leverages time. In this category, you are completely free from the compounding gains and losses that bind paper investments. This means you can quickly earn high rates of return, but the downside is time. Outside of love, time is our most precious resource. You will likely find that with any business you begin, your time is quickly drained. So you must take a long, hard look at your life before embarking down this road. Do you truly have the time and energy it requires to make a go of it? What will your friends and family think? If you're young, you must recognize that you might be placing a portion of your youth on the line. That lost youth represents a vitality that you will never reclaim. Are you really okay with that? What sorts of guardrails can you create to ensure this business does not overtake your entire life? How can you utilize leverage to regain some of that time?

Business entrepreneurship is the only investment category that does not compound from equity. There's no compound return equation involved. And what's really cool is that once you build it up, you can convert into an annuity (a regular cash flow stream). This investment category frees you from those compound return equations that govern the other two investment categories. With the right risk management, you can "fail" and *still* turn a profit. That makes it great for specific life situations. For example, if you are middle-aged with a relatively small savings, moderate earning potential, lots of time, and dislike frugality, then this investment category can generate lots of money very quickly.

GETTING REAL ABOUT DIRECT OWNERSHIP OF REAL ESTATE

The real estate investment category is a leveraged play on inflation. That's another way of saying that when interest rates rise, your mortgage debt declines. Of course that's only helpful if you lock in low interest rates for the long term. The interest rate of your mortgage is as important as the price of your property. But be careful! In this case, the type of leverage is financial leverage, which is always risky. The math we discussed earlier in this chapter shows that financial leverage cuts both ways, which is why some people have lost lots of money in the real estate game. Being overly financially leveraged is the root cause of many people's credit problems.

The key is timing. Since the future is intrinsically unknowable, you must carefully time your purchases to balance the unknowns. If you buy real estate too early in an economic cycle, price declines will put your mortgage under water (meaning you owe more on your mortgage than the value of the property). Depending on the type of property, an economic downturn can result in rent reductions and vacancies. On the other hand, if you buy real estate too late in an economic cycle, you will miss out on the low interest rates required to make the math work in your favor.

Overall, the real estate investment category represents a combination of the paper and business entrepreneurship investment categories, in terms of the underlying math. The upsides to real estate are huge. It takes little cash to get started (compared to paper assets) and little time (compared to business entrepreneurship). In fact, if you're young, you would do well to buy a small apartment building with a fully amortized, fixed rate mortgage. If you live there, you can simultaneously learn the ins and outs of being a landlord, while reaping the associated housing savings and tax benefits. The way the math works, by the time you own three or four buildings, you will most likely have achieved some level of financial independence. Of course, the viability of this scenario will vary widely based on local tenants' rights laws, so do your research.

The unique characteristic of the real estate investment category is that it is illiquid. That's just a fancy way of saying you can't "spend" real estate in the same way you can spend cash in a savings account. Depending on the economic cycle, real estate can be tough to unload. It is historically a low-volatility asset with a high transaction cost, which makes the optimum holding period relatively long (fix and flips not withstanding). Therefore, all your risk management should occur up front, when you are structuring the deal.

The largest potential downside in real estate is the illiquidity of the market during times of credit deflation. If you own your property outright, you will be completely in the clear, because you can just wait for the inevitable market return. But if you're caught over-leveraged during a real estate downturn, you can lose your shirt. The problem is during these periods, supply often exceeds demand to the point that it's impossible to unload your real estate for anything more than rock bottom prices. And if you need cash for any reason, it means you're likely to lose a lot of money when selling your property.

The moral of the story here is to ensure any real estate investment you purchase generates positive cash flow as soon as you close. That way you are paid every month that you own. It also gives you a margin for error. In times of inflation, you'll make buckets of money. In times of deflation, this cash flow will help you weather the storm. Focus on building wealth in real terms, after inflation.

SUMMARY

Financial freedom is really quite simple, although putting the practices into place can take a lifetime of trial and error. Pay down all of your unsecured debt as fast as possible. Create a collaborative plan with your family to save more and spend less in a way that feels like abundance, rather than deprivation. Then invest the difference as wisely as you can, based on your wants, needs, values, and lifestyle.

There is no single best path of investment, nor any one-shoe-fits-all approach. Investing is both an art and a science. The "science" is the underlying math behind each investment category. The "art" is the life you are living, the values you hold dear, and the love that sustains you. That's why it requires your active participation: so you can create a strategy specifically tailored to your needs, and build the life of your dreams, such that you might be of more effective service to others.

CHAPTER 6

FAMILY

For those of us cast aside because of our sexual orientation, "family" can be a loaded word. Once we are excised from the tapestry of our origins, who then are we? How do we make our way in the world alone, when the template of our lives is either missing or only half-complete? Where do we then turn when we reach for home? Who are our sources of wisdom and consolation? Is it fair or even realistic to expect friends to fill that void? Do we hire therapists to raise us and sit with our grief or unattended shame? If family is meant to embody love without end, where do we turn in its absence? To whom do we cling?

This is precisely why coming out can be so gut-wrenching for so many of us; it's also why coming out is a precious gift. It means more people get to see your sweet soul. Your greatest gift to the world is sharing your authentic and unapologetic self. That act alone changes the world. It paves the way for others to come out and bare their souls as well. It removes the shackles of homophobia from your straight loved ones, who may never even have recognized how enslaved they had become by their bigotry. However, the risks are real, and the consequences are potentially devastating. But how sweet the rewards when you feel completely seen and known, and your loved ones still want to invest in all that they see.

Coming out is your gift to give, which means it has to happen on your timeline, when you're ready. The harsh reality is that some of your families will reject you, the way mine rejected me. Moving through the world without family is rough; I won't sugarcoat it. When our families reject us, sometimes we gay men wrap ourselves in the cocoon of primary relationships. We quickly find a lover, and then get too attached too soon, and usually to the wrong person. The allure of our love quickly fades, becomes rife with codependency and enmeshment, ripe for abuse and rejection. At other times, in the absence of family we hide from the world—keeping everyone at arm's length in some misguided attempt at self-protection, desperately trying to prevent the repeat of our core woundedness. We believe the world is profoundly unsafe and people are fundamentally untrustworthy.

Even if we have a family that embraces and celebrates our identities, the world can be a cold and cruel place for gay men. Our loved ones might be shining beacons of light, but into what dark void? How far can their love carry us in the face of all the bigotry and hate that has long been endemic to straight society? How can we thrive, with so many cards stacked against us? The reality is that depending on our age or location, many of us likely hold all sorts of self-limiting beliefs. We censor our dreams, narrowcast, listen to their lies, and internalize their negative messages.

So what are we to do then about family? How do we heal and become whole, and at what cost? These are the big questions in which, as gay men, many of our ideas about family reside. They are questions meant to be lived, not answered. Continuously examined, turned over again and again in gentle curiosity, in honorable meditation and noble silence, as we give back to our community, seek to serve our brothers, and make their way in the world a little less onerous. While we wrestle with the philosophical, we can actively embody the change we would like to see.

Be it your biological family or your family of origin, I encourage you to reach for them only when you long for them: when you miss something that only they can provide, when you want to tap into the full story of your genetic family tree, or experience being part of the whole. Follow your inspired heart and intuition. But remember this: your love is a precious gift and your time is sacred. You don't owe anyone a thing. I don't care if they paid for college, or went to your band concerts. It doesn't matter if they hosted your sleepovers or changed your diapers. Love incurs no debt. Operating out of guilt or obligation is a quick way to derail your sanity. Family drama is just a mask to hide underlying family resentments. You win no gold stars by demonstrating how much you can endure.

GETTING REAL ABOUT YOUR GAY MALE FRIENDS

In the gay community, sometimes our friends become our family, but finding these friends can be challenging. It's no secret that we can be crueler to one another than even our most homophobic bullies. We know all the typical weak spots in other members of our tribe, and sometimes exploit them mercilessly. This dynamic is a form of internalized homophobia, a scrambling for proximal power: I feel better about myself if I put you down. Maybe doing so even helps me curry favor with a straight, cis man or woman. This scenario is particularly common in the workplace, where many of us tend to be our most closeted. But it can happen any time that we exist in a primarily straight space and succumb to greed, jealousy, or envy. In reality, these are all just different flavors of scarcity-based fear.

In groups of gay men, and often in our own spaces, we are prone to cannibalize our own. The core issue is actually one of competition. However if drugs and alcohol are involved, they can exacerbate this dynamic. Maybe we're competing for the attention of a romantic partner, or perhaps just seeking the approval of our friends. Whatever the case, we cut our teeth on one another through insults, bullying, gossip, or other types of emotional violence. And violence is just another way of saying, "I'm all out of ideas." Many of us have spent large parts of our lives outcast, hiding, or ignored. As a result, we might desperately seek approval or attention, whether through outlandish behavior, excess sexual energy, or just plain cruelty. The end result is the same: we try to garner social standing on the backs of our brothers, but just end up lonely and isolated.

Another scenario I've witnessed time and again is the undue sexualization of our own male relationships, whether straight or gay. Either we develop crushes on unattainable guys, or ruin otherwise healthy budding friendships by falling into bed together without clear communication. What each case has in common is the use of that which we most hate about ourselves (our healthy lust for men) as a way to further our shame and loneliness. In our community, there is a long, rich history of lovers becoming friends. Many of us first started this pattern as children, when the world presumed we were straight and required we socialize with those who were actually the objects of our attraction. As adults, straight society disallowed us from congregating in plain sight for decades, and thus forced us into furtive sexual acts. Many of these blossomed into love, while others bloomed into friendship. But that's not what I'm describing here. I'm referring to the behavior (either predatory, casual, or unconscious) of seducing our existing friends, with no sincere intention of emotional intimacy, and no forethought to their well-being.

Each of these scenarios validates a self-destructive belief, which has been indoctrinated upon us by straight society for most of our lives: gay men are fundamentally unloving and unlovable. But of course that's not true. Given enough self-esteem and support, we are just like any other population. We form loving social structures. Sometimes they appear strikingly similar, and sometimes they appear strikingly different to straight social structures. We make no apologies for these differences and distinctions; they are wholly ours. They represent a piece of our culture, which is why it is so important that we resist all homophobia everywhere we meet it, even in our own hearts. We simply cannot afford it. Too many of us are too wounded, too lonely, and too at risk. It is imperative that we take rigorous inventory of our lives and hire the necessary professionals to help us root out our own self-hatred.

Healthy friendships between gay men save lives. They fill a void in our hearts, of which we might not even be aware.

They are fundamental to our health and well-being. Of course, it is also healthy to have a vibrant network of straight friendships. The two groups can coexist in our solar system of relatedness. The more the merrier! Diversity is a strength for everyone, including us. If we only have friendships with one group or another, we should probably inquire about the underlying reasons. There is likely some internalized homophobia at play. Either we reject parts of ourselves (and choose to live primarily in the straight world), or we fear parts of ourselves (and choose to live primarily in the gay world). Balance and equanimity is key, as well as having the backbone to refuse to allow others to define you, your possibilities, or your relationships.

GETTING REAL ABOUT YOUR CHOSEN FAMILY

For gay men, chosen families have been a lifeline for centuries: a replacement for all that was stolen from so many of us, and a support system of our own making. Many members of our chosen family might be former lovers, a dynamic that is fairly unique to gay culture. Other members of our chosen family might be longtime, platonic friends. There are no rules, which is what makes it feel so liberating. But be careful: the empowered, mindful selection of family in and of itself rights no wrongs and heals few wounds. Nor is the mere passage of time an effective balm. Healing our core woundedness requires direct action. This does not diminish the essentiality of our chosen families. However, any harm inflicted by our biological families or families of origin is a separate issue. Meeting that challenge will only make us better friends, lovers, and family members.

When exactly do friends become family? What unseen

bridge is crossed to warrant that word? Is it based on longevity, shared interests, or mutual passion for each other's friendship? I believe that when two souls meet and truly see one another, love happens. Over time, and with great consistency, that love breeds loyalty. And eventually when one is in need, such that the other is inspired to freely extend past their comfort zone in love and support, then something beautiful is born—something for which we have no words. Where love becomes fierce, stories are shared, and lives merge.

Somewhere along this arc, a family is born. But you can see both the irony and the conundrum: though began in shared experiences, the cementing of bonds is often based on need. So we overly guarded gay men, who wrap ourselves in the illusions of control and self-protection, are also smothering our would-be flowering families. It is in our brokenness that we are seen and loved. All that is required from us is vulnerability and faith.

These days, our chosen families are not limited to friend groups. In many countries around the world, gay men can legally marry one another. This monumental step forward represents one of the fastest-evolving, positive social changes in human history. To say that we're still finding our footing is an understatement. The AIDS epidemic wiped out many of our would-be role models, while others were broken by centuries of homophobia. Those of us that have chosen to explore marriage are pioneers of a sort, and frankly we're making things up as we go along. Where does natural human design end, and a patriarchal social structure designed to subjugate women begin? In our rush for equality, are we losing something along the way? Is our participation in this institution something sacred, or just some embodiment of the homophobic messages straight society taught us as children? How do we carve out a space especially for us? What does marriage even mean anymore, other than a vehicle for the various rights that governments have long used to incentivize it? Should government even be in the marriage game? And why is the institution limited to just two participants?

All things being equal, culture always wins. And our culture is still quite primitive. I suspect in the near future the culture of many countries will not see an intrinsic link between two-person marriages and the raising of children. Our culture has already started the process of dropping the forced association of "heterosexual" and child-rearing. I believe family units will soon exist in a panoply of forms. In many cases they already do. So what then of the various associated legal protections? And what happens when families change, or dissolve entirely? These questions demonstrate just how much and how quickly our culture will be required to adapt. Many will feel left behind, and our social divisions will likely continue to deepen in the interim.

Families don't need children as validation. While many long to raise children as an expression of hope and love, others do not. Neither choice is more valid or honorable than the other. There are many heterosexual couples who cannot or choose not to have children. Their relationships are still beautiful and fruitful. There are many gay men choosing to have children as part of their lives. And these days, there are so many ways to accomplish that. Raising children directly is just one of those ways. Educating or volunteering with children is another. Being close to a family with children is a third. You need not be forced into any particular choice.

It is important to acknowledge that many men who identify as gay have biological children resulting from heterosexual relationships. There are all sorts of reasons for this, and these families are no less intrinsically valid, loving, or successful than any other family. When it comes to bringing children into gay homes, there are now more options than ever: fostering, adoption, surrogacy, etc. Of course this doesn't mean the road is free from obstacles and challenges, but we are certainly blessed beyond what any of our elders could have ever dreamed.

GETTING REAL ABOUT MARRIAGE

The fight for marriage equality has been at the heart of the gay rights movement for decades. Depending on when and where you grew up, a legally recognized marriage may not have ever been on your radar. I had always assumed it would be out of reach in my lifetime, and had no emotional attachment to the concept. I had been with my partner for a few years already when Washington State passed a civil unions bill, which at least recognized our relationship within the state. And then one day, amidst a flurry of quick-moving news, we received a letter from the state saying that they were abandoning the civil union designation altogether. Our partnership would be dissolved. We could either get married or not, but we could no longer live with the designation of civil union. With the best of intentions, they just sprung it on us, which I'm sure led to some pretty awkward conversations!

My partner and I had never even discussed marriage, outside of some vague concept in the fight for civil rights. We had never thought through the nuts and bolts of it, or how it might change our relationship. Would we have a ceremony? Would we write vows? What did this all mean? I'm defiant by nature, so a big part of me just wanted to rebel: who is the government to tell me I can or cannot get married? Does this mean we have to get divorced if we split at some point in the future? We ended up deciding to get married, and remain so to this day.

What's so beautiful about marriage equality, aside from all the lovely married gay couples out there, is the fact that gay kids from many countries around the world can dream of one day getting married. They can form the emotional attachments to the concept that I never had. They can play dress up and pretend to walk down the aisle, and over time, they can think through which aspects of the institution are meaningful to them. Since I never got that chance, I tend to focus on the legal rights and tax benefits that my husband and I now enjoy, as well as all the suffering of our ancestors, who never got to experience the reality of this moment.

For those of you that are single adults, now is your time. Just because you didn't necessarily dream of this day as a child, does not mean you cannot start that process now. We as gay men are just not used to having these conversations. It's imperative that we have the courage to chart our own course, create our own vocabulary, and do what's right for us. There are many constraints on the institution of marriage. Just because you seek a marriage license and want to enjoy all the associated legal protections and tax benefits, does not mean you need to mimic heterosexual marriages in every way.

- As a gay couple, how will you merge and protect your various assets?
- What will you call each other, and how will you present your relationship to the world?
- Will one of you take the other's last name? Will you keep your current last names? Will you choose a last name different from what each of you currently use?
- Will you be monogamous (you certainly don't have to be)?
- Will you live together (you certainly don't have to)?
- Will you have children (it's absolutely not required)?
- Will you each continue to work?

There are many questions to consider. But the point is that you have a clean slate, an opportunity to invent something new. Do what feels right for each of you and your relationship, and change things over time, if you choose.

GETTING REAL ABOUT BECOMING A FOSTER PARENT

In some quarters, nothing seems to elicit more panic than placing children in families with gay men. But the truth is, families come in all shapes and sizes, and that diversity is a source of strength. What better way to prepare children for our pluralistic society than to provide them with loved ones from all walks of life? Especially when one of the largest obstacles in foster placement is the availability of loving homes? Gay men deserve the same rights as straight members of society. If you are passionate about having children in your life, please don't allow your past fears or prejudices to stop you from getting informed about all available possibilities.

While there are currently no federal laws in the US explicitly preventing gay men from fostering or adopting a child, either as single men or same-sex couples, please do your research. In the US, all laws are dynamic and subject to a variety of legal challenges from any number of angles. In certain cases, there might also be state and local laws, statutes, or policies, which could complicate your adoption journey. And that's to say nothing of the various agency attitudes or practices on the ground which might severely impact your efforts. Bias and stigma prevent so many wonderful gay men from becoming wonderful gay fathers. And while there is absolutely no reason for you to yield to these self-limiting beliefs, it is critical you get informed, so you can be as empowered as possible to advocate for you and your family.

It's also important to consider the support of your family. Extended family networks often play a huge role in the lives of children. From sharing intergenerational family knowledge, to providing additional role models, to free babysitting, the love of your family and/or your partner's family can make a profound difference when it comes to your child. If you anticipate this support will not be there, be honest about if and how you will be able to fill that void. Perhaps you have a strong friend network. Perhaps you can plug into an association of other parents. In most cases, it will be best for you and your child if you are both surrounded by a full system of love and support.

You might face skepticism from your friends or family about wanting to be a parent. Some of them might never have considered the fact that gay people can even have children. Many times, being a man seems to heighten this issue, thanks to our society's outdated gender norms. In other cases, your friends may not know how to relate to kids. Maybe they think children are boring, or that as new parents you will cramp their lifestyle. That's okay. You don't have to make anybody right or wrong. There are plenty of places you can turn to for support, and you can always make new friends. The friends that love you truly and deeply will support you and stick with you. The friends on your periphery that float away for a time might even come back into your life one day, perhaps when they become parents themselves!

When you apply to become a foster parent in the US, expect the agency to require you to attend weeks of preparatory classes, host home visits from their agents, and scrutinize your life. It's all in the name of evaluating your ability to provide a safe and loving temporary home for a foster child, before granting you an official foster parent license. Most agencies will also likely stress to you that your goal at this point is to become a great foster parent, not an adoptive parent. Many children in the foster care program will never become available for adoption at all. The entire goal for the foster agency is the child's reunification with their biological family. Yes, sometimes these situations change and can become permanent. However, if you go into the foster care process with that dream in mind, you are setting everyone up for disappointment.

Once licensed, you might receive an availability call much more quickly than you ever dreamed. Some foster parents receive that call within hours of being licensed, some receive it within weeks. Every situation is different; your flexibility will be key to maintaining your sanity and well-being. Some of you will be used to spending time with children. But for others, this will all be very new. Those of you in this second group might feel a little freaked out at first. That's okay. It's completely normal to feel scared of such a large responsibility. Foster parents are real parents. The often-temporary nature of these arrangements does not negate the loving care and concern that foster parents provide to children. Remember you are not alone. You have support. You can do this. Parents learn to do this every day, and you can too. Your sexual orientation has no impact on your aptitude to learn and practice positive parenting skills.

GETTING REAL ABOUT ADOPTION

Government child welfare agencies seek primarily to reunite children with members of their biological family. The fact that a child is available for adoption means one of three things: there is no family, the family has chosen to place them into adoption, or a government agency has deemed that the family lacks the capacity to raise the children themselves.

In some cases, children enter the adoption process after sustained abuse or neglect. These situations can lead to learning disabilities, attachment disorders, or developmental disabilities. This is where some gay men might actually have a parenting advantage. Many gay men know what it's like to grow up with additional challenges. They enter the adoption process with a greater level of empathy, understanding, and resiliency than many straight people. Gay men can then use these qualities for the betterment of their parenting skills. So don't ever let anyone tell you that, as a gay man, you are somehow intrinsically unqualified to be a parent.

When you contact an agency seeking to enter the adoption process, you can expect them to send you to classes. There you will learn more about the process, hear general information about typical adoptees, and get the chance to meet other prospective adoptive parents. You will then likely complete an in-depth initial application, which includes an interview. During this interview, the screeners will try to assess your potential ability to provide positive therapeutic parenting (that type of parenting that creates feelings of safety in traumatized children). Nobody expects you to be an expert; they are just assessing your aptitude, affinity, passion, and stability for loving a child who has likely been through a tough time.

In most cases, both your initial application and the screeners' comments will comprise your official adoption application. You will then be required to go before an official adoptive parent approval panel to discuss your application. Expect lots of tough questions, especially as (a) gay prospective parent(s). It would not be unusual to be asked to discuss your current and anticipated support structure, your financial stability, your approach to parenting children of different genders, and potentially how you would parent children of different races or ethnicities. These are purposefully tough questions, not meant to trick you or catch you off guard, but because this is a sacred, soul-searching process.

Your ability to parent is not constrained by your sexual orientation. Gay men can do everything that straight men can do. Feminine men can father just as well as masculine men. And dads can do just about everything that moms can do. But there is another dynamic here that is important to acknowledge. If you are a gay man or couple adopting a female child, you will need additional support. Most men do not have a female perspective on the world. For instance, other than some trans men, most men have never had a menstrual cycle. Most men have no idea what it's like to communicate with women, when men are not in the room. Having a diverse support network is crucial. You can turn to women for advice, and even ask they spend time with your children. These extended chosen family members can be huge assets in your child's life. Trying to do this alone is a disservice to everyone.

The same is true for anyone adopting a child of a different race or ethnicity. You can absolutely have a beautiful experience and raise a wonderful family in these situations, but it will require more awareness. In some cases, this will also mean navigating a more complex legal path, especially if it involves adopting a child from a different country. Here are some things you will need to consider:

- If you are a white man or couple, who is going to teach your child of color how to live in a racist society?
- Does your support network contain enough racial diversity to support your child's growth and experience?
- Have you ever spent time with children of different races or ethnicities?
- As a white man or couple, are you ready for the bigotry your family is likely to encounter, especially since it is unlikely that you have ever personally experienced racial animus?
- If you are a person or couple of color (or of mixed races or ethnicities) and adopting a child the world perceives as white, are you ready to endure new and different forms of racism?

- Does your adoptive child speak English? Or do you speak their native language? If not, how will you bridge that gap?

All of these questions can be answered and these issues overcome. But you will need to face them openly, honestly, and head-on. Families of blended races and ethnicities endure so much bigotry and bias, and it is important to acknowledge that before a child is placed in your home. You will likely be asked all of these questions by the adoption agency panel anyway, so you might as well start your soul searching now.

Adopting children who have mental or physical disabilities can introduce additional complexities as well. Ask yourself:

- Is your home accommodating to their special needs?
- Do you have access to extra support and resources to help you navigate the mental or physical healthcare system?
- Have you ever spent time with any children that have special needs?

You can absolutely learn and prepare for this experience, but it is imperative to enter this process fully informed. There are numerous resources out there to help you, based on the specifics of your situation. Every child deserves a family that is both loving and well-prepared.

After the adoption agency panel approves your application, you will then enter the placement process. For many adoptive parents, this phase can be the most grueling step in their journey. It is at this stage that you are most likely to encounter institutionalized bigotry. Many agencies are still aligned with religious organizations, and bias is sometimes explicitly part of their charter. Be prepared.

This part of the process sometimes feels like you are being asked to hurry up and wait. Some couples get placed within hours of their applications, while others wait months. The whole process can seem so random, as you navigate the Byzantine requirements and wait for the magic phone call telling you that a child is ready to be placed in your home. In general, it is impossible to predict what you will face over the course of the adoption process; no two situations are the same. A certain amount of humor and equanimity will serve you well, as you try to roll with the punches.

In some cases, you will be placed with a child who is currently residing with a foster family. The easiest transitions are those in which the adoptive family and the foster family share values and can remain in contact. It's even better if the birth family can retain some level of contact over the long run. This way, your child has a full sense of themselves, their story, and their place in the world. Keep an open and loving heart, with the child's best interests in mind.

GETTING REAL ABOUT SURROGACY

Gay men have more options than ever before in having genetic connections with their babies. In Vitro Fertilization (IVF) and surrogacy are quickly becoming mainstream for both HIV+ and HIV- gay men. But it's still important that you do your homework.

Here's how the IVF and surrogacy process typically works:

1. You (or you and your partner) provide sperm to a fertility clinic.
2. A woman (not necessarily the gestational carrier) donates her eggs.
3. The fertility clinic inseminates the woman's eggs in order to create viable embryos.
4. The fertility clinic implants the embryos in the gestational carrier (not necessarily the egg donor).

That means, as part of this process, you will be selecting the following:

- Surrogacy Agency
- Fertility Clinic
- Egg Donor
- Gestational Carrier

Surrogacy agencies in the US are largely unregulated. That means it's very important to educate yourself on industry best practices when choosing an agency. Any reputable agency should pre-screen all surrogacy candidates for the following:

- A thorough psychological evaluation of both the gestational carrier candidate and her partner (if applicable).
- Credit check of both the gestational carrier candidate and her partner (if applicable).
- Criminal background check of both the gestational carrier candidate and her partner (if applicable).
- Home visits with the gestational carrier candidate to ensure she will be living in a safe, clean, and comfortable environment during the gestation period.
- An examination of the gestational carrier candidate's

obstetric history, to ensure there are no red flags or past pregnancy complications.

When the agency presents the gestational carrier candidate to a fertility clinic for a potential candidate screening, you will want to know that the agency has done everything in its power to ensure the fertility clinic will feel comfortable about working with her.

In addition to getting to know gestational carrier candidates, any surrogacy agency you hire should also be getting to know you. They should ask you some of the following questions:

- What are your values?
- What are you seeking in a carrier?
- How many embryos would you like to have transferred?
- How many children do you envision having (are you hoping that the carrier might one day carry additional children for you)?

The agency you hire should make every attempt to match you with someone that shares your values. It is critical to establish such topics as selective reduction and termination of a pregnancy if the baby is unhealthy, up front. You cannot legally force women to comply with your requests, so it's important to be on the same page as much as possible.

Selecting a fertility clinic is another critical step in the process. You will want to ensure that you select a research-oriented clinic with a high success rate. As a gay man, you will want to ensure the clinic you select is gay-friendly, with a focus on surrogacy, and has significant experience with gestational carrier cycles.

This pathway to parenthood is the most financially expensive. Not only are you paying all the agency expenses, but you must often buy insurance for both the egg donor and the surrogate, as well as cover their lost wages. There are often ancillary medical expenses you will be expected to help cover as well—everything from naturopathic treatments to nutritional supplements. You can often expect to pay over $100k, depending on where and when you begin this process, and insurance coverage (or lack thereof) can vary widely. At the end of these treatments, not all would-be parents end up with a baby.

HIV+ gay men can absolutely have a genetic connection to their baby. If you are HIV+, your surrogacy journey is not all that different from an HIV- man. Thankfully, many fertility clinics in the US are very welcoming to HIV+ men of all sexual orientations; this should absolutely be part of your criteria when you research prospective clinics. These clinics will often recommend that HIV+ men work with special programs that specialize in the transmission of HIV through semen. These steps can ensure that any semen used to create embryos in a participating clinic are free of HIV, so that the virus is not passed to the child.

SUMMARY

Family is a crucial and multi-faceted topic for gay men, especially given our current loneliness epidemic. Family does not just refer to the group into which you were born, or those who raised you. It can refer to anybody with whom you share your life. Your family is comprised of those loved ones who know and hold your story, whose love sustains you, and who have your best interests at heart. Your family inspires you to do your greatest good, walks with you for a lifetime, and claims you as one of their own. This group can be made up of your friends, former lovers, distant relatives, biological family, family of origin, or some combination.

You get to make the rules together. Nobody gets to dictate to you what your family should look like. Stay empowered. Fight for your love and relationships, and grow your love as much as you can. In some cases, that might mean getting legally married, so you can enjoy all the associated rights and privileges. But you certainly don't have to. Your love is no less worthy if it's not sponsored by the government. In addition to its problematic history, there are constraints on the legal institution of marriage that will make it distasteful to some.

Extending your loving family might mean having children. In this day and age, there are numerous ways to have children in your life: volunteering, mentoring, spending time with the children of loved ones, fostering, adoption, or surrogacy, just to name a few. While all laws are dynamic, there are no current laws in most Western countries that prevent gay men from participating in the lives of children. As always, the key is to figure out what you want. Then get informed, so you can take charge and make the decisions that will help you build the family of your dreams. Because when it comes to family, the stakes are too high to defer to the bigotry and preconceived notions of others.

CHAPTER 7

FRIENDS

My family raised me to be isolated and subservient, to define my worth by my usefulness. Society reinforced this distorted thinking through an unrelenting homophobia. It required I don masks, detach from hope, and dissociate from the world. Each personal interaction was fraught with peril and brought the potential for battle. As a result, I never allowed myself to be seen and known, to step out of the bunker and leave the garrison, or to set down my sword and take off my armor. Eventually, I lost my taste for the milk of human kindness altogether.

I was an only child, which exacerbated my loneliness. My father had only a minimal presence in my life. There was nobody to teach me how to be a man, much less a gay man. There was nobody to model male friendship after, nobody to ruffle my feathers and challenge me. My negative thoughts became patterns, and my patterns became core beliefs, until my whole world was the sum of the stories I'd spun.

In the aftermath, I've spent my life just guessing at normal. I had to make it all up as I went along: how to set down the shackles of homophobia, how to love and support people with healthy boundaries, and most importantly, how to cultivate relationships based on mutual joy, rather than just our shared suffering. Were it not for the support of paid professionals and the wisdom I found in literature, I would have been irrevocably lost long ago.

And I'm not alone. Little in the lives of gay men is more challenging than the forging and nurturing of sustainable friendships, that realm where our interior worlds meet, and our inner monologues are made manifest. It is through friendships that our stories first touch. This also makes it a wonderful opportunity to practice love, inclusion, and acceptance. It is through friendships that we can ferret out and confront our lingering or latent biases, set down our fetishes and issues of objectification, and then improve. This is the basis of the contemporary Progressive Movement in US politics: the idea that while nobody is perfect, when we know better, we can do better. And do better we must, if we are to experience the togetherness our hearts crave.

Making friends is all about human connection—abandoning our assumptions and setting down our preconceived notions. Doing so enables us to see others as they truly are, rather than who we think they might be, or wish they were. Friendship is a lovely mixture of fun and selflessness; the combination of common interests with the wanting of what's best for one another. If two friends enjoy the same hobby, but one is not free, then the love is lacking, hobbies be damned. True friendship requires more. Really seeing someone requires an acknowledgment of any power imbalances, whether due to systemic racism, sexism, homophobia, ableism, classism, ageism, or any other bias. True friendship calls us to begin the work of radical inclusion, the dismantling of all institutionalized othering, as well as its resulting theft. For if we are unequal, our friendship can only go just so far.

GETTING REAL ABOUT GAY RACISM

White, cis men living in the US have more privilege than just about any social group on the planet. Privilege refers to our unearned advantages. It's not that white, cis men necessarily have easy lives; it's that their lives are not made more difficult by virtue of their race or gender. Put another way, privilege is when you think something is not a problem, simply because it's not a problem for you personally. Society often deems gay, white, cis men as white and male first. That means we have undue access to proximal power. That power is undue because it is not based on anything we have earned, and it's proximal because it requires cozying up to society's true masters: straight, white, cis men. Those of us who benefit from the lie of whiteness have the obligation to do more than simply not be racist. We must be explicitly anti-racist, and push back with all our love and might against systemic racial bias and bigotry.

It does not fall on the shoulders of people of color (POC) to fight this fight. That's our work as white people. In the same way it is the responsibility of straight people to lead the charge against homophobia; that's their work. It is the responsibility of men to fight misogyny, the work of the able-bodied to fight discrimination of the disabled, and on, and on. If we are coming from a place of love, we must wield our power in the service of the disenfranchised. Anything else is just delusion or greed. Gay white men do not get a free pass on fighting racism simply because we've known bigotry.

Sometimes the legacy of systemic, intergenerational racial bigotry seems insurmountable. It's tempting to hope that someone else will magically fix everything for us. But here's what we white people can do:

- **Acknowledgement:**
  - We must acknowledge that racism exists, and that no part of it is the fault of POC.
  - We must acknowledge that we as white people will probably never have any clue what it feels like to live in the US as part of a racial minority.
  - We must acknowledge that the effects of racism are real and often devastating, and that we white people benefit from structural racism in ways we likely don't even understand.
- **Willingness:**
  - We must cultivate a continual willingness to have scary conversations about structural racism with other white people.
  - We must create space to fully listen to the stories of POC.
  - We must risk our privilege and discomfort to challenge racial bias and bigotry wherever and whenever we encounter it, even in our own homes or places of employment.
- **Advocacy:**
  - We must explicitly advocate for POC in all walks of life.

- We must vote for POC.
- We must shop at minority-owned businesses.
- We must engage with minority-driven art, theater, and music.
- We must hire POC.
- We must date POC. Not just because they are POC, but because that is the natural consequence of seeing anyone as they truly are, in their wholeness and individuality.

- **Humility:**
  - We must meditate on and search the various ways we have fetishized or rejected POC, based solely on their race (and often under the guise of preference).
  - We must commit to celebrating racial diversity while seeing people as unique individuals.
  - We must get to know the person behind the race and allow them to get to know us. This is emotional intimacy.

If you struggle to find friends, I encourage you to consider any conscious or unconscious biases ("preferences") that might be influencing your choices. Maybe your next friend won't look like you thought! The bottom line is that unless and until we white people dismantle systemic racism, many of our gay brothers will not truly be free. That means none of us will be free. We can do this. We must do this, for ourselves and each other, in the name of friendship.

GETTING REAL ABOUT GAY MISOGYNY

I think most homophobia is based on some form of sexism: any self-serving, outdated, or misguided ideas about gender roles, norms, or expressions. This evil does not just impact women. There is pressure on all men (and especially gay men) from straight society to conform to those behaviors currently deemed masculine. This pressure can infect our friendships. It can cause us to seek out those we deem more "manly," while labeling others as "flamers" or "too gay." Many of us lie to ourselves about how even though we're gay, we're not *that* gay, and that our sexuality is just a small part of our lives. We modify our behavior to "pass" within straight society. We shame "bottoms" for being sexually subservient.

We fetishize or fear those whose body parts we claim don't match their gender. The inconvenient truth is that some women have penises, some women have vaginas, some women have both, and some women have neither. Part of the wondrous mystery of life is that nature remains stubbornly unconcerned with our social constructs. There is no single way to embody the masculine or feminine. In fact, those culturally constituted norms are entirely fluid. And more importantly, our dignity cannot be measured by something as small as a pronoun.

Not only is this internalized homophobia injurious to our mental health and well-being, but it limits our potential friendships and perpetuates bigotry. Here are some things we can do to fight this:

- Fight sexism:
    - We must refuse to participate in the beauty myth that society inflicts on women, in order to reduce their power and take their money. One way we can do this is by refraining from publicly commenting on their appearance. If you want to celebrate a woman's

appearance, choose your words wisely. Select terms that empower them.

- We must treat women as intellectual equals and workplace peers.
- We must refuse to use language about women that shames their bodies or sexual behaviors.
- We must help empower women to participate in whatever culture they choose, even if that culture is based on modesty.
- We must stop expressing public disgust at female bodies.

- Fight misogyny:
  - We must refuse to label anybody's behaviors in gendered terms. These evaluations are culturally constituted, and typically carry disempowering baggage. To refer to someone's behavior as "feminine" rarely increases their social power or standing.
  - If you don't like the tone of someone's voice, the way they stand, or how they move their hands, then simply keep those judgments to yourself. You would do well to look inward and ask yourself where these judgements originate. We must seek ways to set them aside and embrace everyone's differences, even if it feels awkward.
  - We must make it a point to cultivate friendships with women and "feminine" gay men (as based on their own labeling of themselves).

- Signal safety and affirmation:
  - Regardless of your culture or sexual orientation, we must implicitly and explicitly indicate our support for women in all their forms, shapes, and sizes.
  - We must learn the language of empowerment.
  - We must publicly support organizations that fight

for equality and the autonomy of women over their bodies and lives.

- We must positively affirm our friendship and allyship.
- We must risk discomfort and power by taking public stands for the empowerment of women and gay men (fight bigotry in the workplace, push back on sexist comments and biases, etc.).

There is so much bias in our society; none of us are free from its impact and effects. Although gay men have a long, rich cultural history of befriending women, we must acknowledge our equally long track record of misogyny. Just as we don't want to be the accessories conveniently adorning the arms of straight women, they don't want to be our accessories either.

We are all fully realized, adult human beings: complex, mysterious, irrational, mercurial, and beautiful. It can be so tempting to gobble up the crumbs of proximal power from the straight male world, at the expense of our female or feminine loved ones. But that behavior hinders us all. It's critical that we explicitly make anti-misogynist choices in all aspects of our lives, in order to create the requisite space to allow our female friends to rise to their full potential and explore all their opportunities. Only then can we truly claim to be their friends.

GETTING REAL ABOUT ECONOMIC DIFFERENCES

It can be downright challenging to be friends with those of different financial means. How can we hope to keep up with friends of greater means? If they have less, how do we avoid fears of exploitation? Our society is not constructed to support mixed-class relationships. Capitalism was designed to create winners and losers, and then market each of them products. It can take a lot of effort and soul searching to transcend these social barriers. We often live in different neighborhoods, have different cultural reference points, and even speak different languages or slang. Our varying opportunities often yield disparate experiences. There are many Americas.

Here are some things we can do to embrace our economic differences:

- **Fight regressive economic policies:** If we are blessed to have the means to support our families, it's important to acknowledge that our fortunes came on the shoulders of (and likely at the expense of) others. In the US, we have numerous policies that adversely impact the poor as a percentage of income, such as transportation taxes and fees, food and beverage taxes, etc. We must explicitly work against these policies—not only to promote equality, but to signal safety and inclusion to our friends living with lower incomes.
- **Pay our own way:** Except in special circumstances, we are probably best served by refraining from borrowing money from our friends. Money comes with too much baggage in our culture, and this behavior can exacerbate power imbalances that erode trust. If we have the means to give money, we can do so as a gift, as opposed to a loan. That means we offer our money for fun and for free, with no strings attached, and no expectations. If we lack the means to participate in an activity with friends, let's just be honest about it. These conversations can be awkward and embarrassing, but what's the alter-

native? True friendship is based on honest and open communication.

- **Refrain from snobbery and class-based comments:** It's hurtful to make broad, sweeping statements about large groups of people. We must treat people as individuals and celebrate diversity. A great way to signal our love and acceptance is to spend time with our friends in their homes, regardless of their wealth or lack of wealth. That includes hugging their kids, eating their food, and playing with their pets.

It's crucial to remember that friendship is not a meritocracy. It's about fun and love and connection. You attract friends by sharing yourself, not by sharing your résumé. Straight society devalues gay friendship. It tells us we are unworthy of love, which can make it tempting to try and "win" friends through achievement. But this impulse is based on the faulty premise that we are not intrinsically deserving of love. It also creates unhealthy dynamics of competition and resentment, which can poison any new and growing relationship.

GETTING REAL ABOUT FRIENDSHIPS WITH OTHER GAY MEN

Ironically, friendships among gay men can be the toughest to sustain. You would think we would easily understand one another, having shared similar stories in many cases. But the reality is that the closet has distorted our experiences, opportunities, and worldviews. Too often we judge other gay men based on their appearances. Yes, pretty privilege is alive and well in the gay community. Not only are we saturated in media images that celebrate youth and thinness, but we have the added burden of being an overly sexualized segment of an already overly sexualized culture. There are just so few of us, and we have been so persecuted.

For centuries, we met quickly and furtively to satisfy our sexual needs, never dreaming we might know real intimacy or lasting love. Over time, this dynamic led to a culture based primarily on appearance and the quest to find those with mutually satisfying sexual behaviors. Cruising was the search for someone who looked like what we wanted and was into what we were. Part of the allure was its secrecy and danger, but also its lack of intimacy. Through a variety of locations, behaviors, and clothing, we sorted ourselves into subgroups, a sort of gay taxonomy, which allowed us to skip the step of actually getting to know one another.

This behavior might be well and good in some spheres of our lives, but when it encroaches on our romantic lives or platonic relationships, it likely gets in the way. Our friends need not participate in our fetishes, but too many of us want to run in packs, "twinning" as it were. We hope that by surrounding ourselves with others who look and act like us, we will facilitate our next hook-up, or at least feel safe. That may be true, but something is lost if our friendship is contingent upon a set list of superficial wants and needs.

Of course, not all romantic feelings are purely sexual. In some cases, our hearts get so full when we spend time with our friends that our feelings grow in depth and intensity. Even if we don't fall into bed together, we might cultivate romantic fantasies. A crush is just a sweet, unrequited attraction. It is perfectly normal and healthy, but like anything, it can get out of balance. Eventually most of us will tire of loving and longing from afar, and we will grow into a need for reciprocal relationships. But in some cases, our hearts can get stuck. We develop patterns of fantasizing about our friends—bouncing from one romantic entanglement to the next, always wanting what we cannot have, so we never need experience the vulnerability of mutual attraction and shared love.

It's natural for gay men to develop crushes on our friends, especially considering the pent-up desire preserved in our hearts from a lifetime of being excluded from the normal adolescent rites of passage reserved for straight society. While straight children were exploring different styles and avenues of relatedness, many gay children were focusing on hiding who we were. It's perfectly understandable that we might experience a somewhat delayed adolescence. This issue is magnified given the often-blurred boundaries between friends and lovers in gay culture.

The key is awareness and communication. If you find yourself crushing on a friend, the first step is to be honest with yourself. Ask yourself these questions:

- Are you interested in pursuing a romantic relationship with this person? Friends often become lovers, and lovers often grow into more formal relationships. But is that what you really want? If so, why? Are you willing to risk losing a friend down the line, if your romantic relationship sours? Lovers can certainly become friends, but often the drama involved in that transition derails the relationship.
- Do you have a pattern of falling in love with (or sexualizing) your friends? If so, then you are likely not seeing

the other person in all their humanness. This is a big red flag. It might be ultimately more loving to first address the pattern with a paid professional, before exploring any romantic feelings with your friend.

- Is your friend available for a romantic relationship? One of the wonderful things about our community is our liberation from heteronormative life scripts. There are no rules to our relationships, other than honesty and selfless love. It does not necessarily matter if your friend already has a significant other in their life (maybe they're open to a third partner, for instance). But have they indicated to you a receptiveness to more romantic love? If not, then you might be placing them in an awkward position by expressing your feelings. Perhaps it would be more loving just to allow your crush to pass.
- Would you prefer to allow your crush to cool? Often these situations seem to resolve of their own accord. But sometimes we can feel stuck by these romantic feelings and afraid that they might undermine our friendship. Hiring a paid professional can be a great way to get some tailor-made strategies to help you move through these feelings. But in the meantime, I encourage you to broaden your view of the object of your crush. Focus on seeing all of their humanness, including what is best for them. Then consider any other areas of your life that you might be avoiding. Instead of indulging the kinds of fantasies that might strengthen your crush, focus on work, hobbies, dating available guys, and spending time with other friends.

Seeing the world through a purely romantic or sexual filter distorts our vision and behavior. It limits our experiences and points of connection, restrains the limits of our love, and hollows us out from the inside. Our friends are not props. I encourage you to refrain from initiating friendships based solely on appearance, especially if you are doing so in order to improve your social standing or access to other men. If your relationships lack intimacy, you might examine their transactional nature. Do you both play with and support each other? Laugh and love? Can you truly count on one another? Our hearts are muscles that require exercise. We must continually go to the places that scare us, challenge our unconscious biases, give until it hurts, and lift others up.

GETTING REAL ABOUT FRIENDSHIPS WITH STRAIGHT, CIS MEN

Some of us have struggled in any capacity to walk with straight, cis men. Let's face it: many of them have broken our trust, over and over. Many of them have beaten and ridiculed us, stolen our money and our opportunities, trampled our hearts, and kicked us out of our families. And yet it is unfair to paint them all with the same brush. Like any collection of people, straight cis men are all individuals, with unique stories that deserve to be heard. Many of them would love us, given half a chance. If we gay men really want to be free from homophobia, we must first transcend it. We must get curious, rise above our wounds, and extend our hearts to the places that scare us. The collective karma of straight, cis men need not preclude our love and friendship.

The love I feel for the straight, cis men in my life is rooted in the present. It has nothing to do with amends or reparations, and requires no reciprocity. I adore them because that's merely what happens when souls come into contact:

hearts get full, regardless of sexual or gender orientation. To my surprise, it turns out I have the capacity to selflessly love straight men. I can release them and release me, hold their fears, and nurture their pain. I can stand tall next to them, and take up space. I can look them in their eyes, and let them melt in my arms. No agenda, no expectations, no resentments. Just their gentle sobs, as they wrestle with the tyranny of their fathers, and navigate the treacherous waters of this new world.

Oh what wreckage they have wrought! And how like little boys they cling, utterly bewildered, unable to hold any of it. These burly men run riot, presuming dominion over everyone, expecting each day to be a halcyon, while trampling tenderness and self-expression. The one true aristocracy, enslaved by their privilege as they burn the world, embers softening to ash. How could I but reach for them, these fresh foals? Pull them close as they squirm, clutching their plights and their slights, wretched and wriggling. Having never known a bad day, but now forced to learn how to suffer. How could I not hold their fragile fingers, as their knock knees tremble? Those that long to find their way, but lug their patrimony like a yolk, nose running, choking on their obligations.

There's no magic formula for forgiveness, and nothing shall be forgotten. But how could I not be moved by their seeping expectations, spoiling in the sun? Bedeviled by this world that they inherited. And damn it if my heart is not called. What they've done is so very real, and yet in some way they're just beholden to patterns, like I've been beholden to patterns, tugging us forth into some collective psychosis. Are we really so different? And if in some small measure I might meet myself in their eyes, and somehow feel healed, why would I deny either of us the pleasure? If I might find some way to share a laugh at our mutual frailties, how could I resist? And so I happily hug their necks and tuck them in. Check their closets and search under their beds. Hold their little hands. Kiss their soft brows. Such that they might never know what I have known. And live free one day to teach their children.

GETTING REAL ABOUT CODEPENDENCY

Codependency is one of those words we like to throw around without considering its meaning. It is an excessive emotional reliance on another person. That person can be a friend, a loved one, a family member, or anyone else in your life. For most people, this reliance begins in childhood. If we grew up with adverse childhood experiences (ACEs), or lived in a dysfunctional family, our emotional self might have formed in a chaotic or unpredictable environment. We might not have experienced the necessary support to form a healthy attachment or identity to our primary care givers. Perhaps they were emotionally or physically abusive. Maybe they were manipulative or blaming. But whatever ACEs we endured, we likely developed a range of coping mechanisms: tactics that in some cases kept us alive. But as we matured, these tactics no longer served us. Codependency makes up just one set of potential responses that we might have employed.

Maybe we became caretakers of the adults in our lives, and now we have a pattern of caretaking other adults, to ensure they need and love us. Perhaps we learned as a child that by being a people-pleaser we could win the love of others, and now we have continued that pattern in our adult lives. Maybe we were manipulated as children into feeling guilty for circumstances beyond our control, and now we have a pattern of feeling guilty as an adult, even when it's unwarranted. Maybe we now have a pattern of distrusting others because we learned as a child that the adults in our lives were untrustworthy. Whatever our story or pattern, it can be rewritten or broken. And in many cases, in order to cultivate healthy adult friendships, it must be. But the good news is that there are tools available to help us. Breaking free of these stories and patterns is a skill, not a talent. That means it can be learned, practiced, and honed.

Many gay men self-sabotage their friendships. Codependency is just one set of patterns we've used to create the self-fulfilling prophecy that those in our tribe are not to be trusted, are not deserving of love, or any of the other stories we have spun to keep us alone. I believe we have used technology (in particular, social media) to magnify these patterns. One pattern that I witness time and again is the comparison of our insides to someone else's outsides, typically their social media profile. It's like I'm comparing my worst day with their best day, or my failures with their successes. It's an uneven playing field. In fact, the most efficient way to be cruel to ourselves is to compare ourselves to others. But if we're going to do this, then let's do it right. When we examine the accomplishments of past luminaries, like Mozart, Mendelssohn, or Newton, there's just no way any of us could hope to stack up. The best thing we can do is throw up our hands, have a good laugh, and delight in our limits.

If you really want to make friends fast, your best bet is to lead with your faults and learn to laugh at yourself. I have found that others gravitate to those who make them feel good about themselves, and the best way to do that is to lightheartedly display your vulnerable humanity in all its faults and glory. Just be yourself! This puts people at ease, because it is a display of confidence and authenticity. It shows an attractive level of self-acceptance. So the next time you're feeling insecure, just embrace it. Say something silly. Do something weird. Those qualities are all real aspects, alive in each of us. Avoiding them indicates a certain amount of self-loathing, a lack of confidence and self-esteem. Like it or not, most people are just not attracted to those qualities. Most of us want to celebrate life and each other, which is why most sustained friendships tend to involve an associated amount of sustained joy.

A flip side of this coin is gravitating to people you want to fix. There is no greater act of interpersonal hubris than in judging someone to be lacking, and then riding in on your white horse to "help." Even if you are somehow successful in helping, you will likely create a dynamic that hinders your friend from standing on their own. Friendship is not about flipping on life's light switches for one another. The best course of action we can undertake for any friend in need is simply to listen, empathize, direct them to professional help, and then stand by them. Anything else will lead us dangerously close to codependency. True interdependency requires healthy boundaries. So if you're struggling to make friends, one indirect procedure you might investigate is the identification and cultivation of those interpersonal boundaries that will support budding relationships.

If you think you might be experiencing some obstacles

preventing you from manifesting the quantity or quality of friendships you desire, the single best thing you can do is hire an expert. That expert can be a therapist, a life coach, a mentor, etc. It can be investing in a personal growth and development retreat or workshop. There are so many modalities out there. The path you choose is not that important; just choose something, and then commit to it. And if it doesn't work, choose something else and then commit to that. If you lack the means to hire someone, you might have to get creative. There are numerous services available to folks living with a low income or strapped for cash. But you are your own best advocate and must make the choice to find the solution that works for you. Nobody can do it for you.

GETTING REAL ABOUT MAKING FRIENDS

Once we've done the personal growth and development work required to be a good friend, the best way we can meet new people is simply by living our lives. Finding new friends is not like applying for a job: we are unlikely to win new ones by "interviewing" them. Real, authentic relationships cannot be forced or rushed. They grow of their own accord, on their own timelines. So our most effective strategy is simply to be ourselves, do the things we love, and allow the magic to happen. Of course that means we need to get out there, into the stream of life. Most of us won't meet anyone by sitting alone on our couches.

The key is to live our best lives, without concern for any outcomes, such that we might attract like-minded people. Then we can explore the exchange of energy with these budding friendships while engaging in any number of life-enhancing activities. I have found equanimity and nonattachment to be much more effective than seeking a specific type of person, and then wrangling them into a friendship. As hearts get close, there is a natural unfolding of any relationship. When we cease to engineer specific outcomes, we open ourselves to the mystery of life and love, and to the nascent opportunities embedded in every moment. This is the fertile ground in which new friendships flower.

Here are some quick ideas to meet like-minded people:

- Volunteer for an organization that means something special to you, but make sure your work is social in nature (it's difficult to make new friends volunteering from your home, online relationships not withstanding).
- Join a sports league. Extra points for trying a new sport. This will keep you from getting caught up in competition. Even more points for signing up for a sport that is lighthearted or silly for everyone involved, like dodgeball or kickball.
- Take a class. Again, try something new, such as a foreign language or pottery. These classes are great, because they typically involve a social element.
- Sign up for extra activities doing something you already love. Perhaps your favorite yoga studio is leading a special class or weekend retreat. These opportunities give you the chance to meet people who can match your passion in a particular area.

Whatever you do, do it with joy. Be yourself. When we open our hearts to the present moment and allow our true selves to shine through, happiness is our natural state. So let go of any need to impress anyone or compete. Release your stories about winning or losing. Don't miss the forest for the trees. Remember, the main point of this endeavor is to experience and manifest joy and fun. If you can do that, people will be attracted to you like a magnet, and they will clamor for your friendship!

For many of us in the gay community, cultivating emerging friendships or nurturing existing friendships can be perilous and confusing. Social isolation and homophobia have often distorted our expectations. Mature adult friendships are different than those we experienced in childhood, adolescence, or young adulthood. Depending on your season of life, friendship might look very different than you remember or imagine. For instance, I'm in my mid-forties, so I don't have the same capacity to sit around for hours, musing about life and the universe, that I did in my twenties.

My friendships today largely involve shared interests in activities (sports, travel, writing, etc.), common professions, and getting together for dinner or drinks with longtime loved ones. It's unrealistic to expect others to have the flexibility to drop everything at a moment's notice, just to go hang out. We all have full lives, so the added richness of friendship takes planning. It's a mutual commitment to carve out space in our calendars, so we can share in what and who we love. It rarely just happens, like it did when we were younger. Sure, we all love to share in a spontaneous adventure with our friends, but these outings are special in part because they are so rare. I'm sure as heck not going to count on a friend's random availability to fulfill my need for love and connection.

The intensity of my friendships has also waned over time.

As we age, most of us just don't have the energy or inclination for deep, emotional sharing or processing with our friends. We hear and hold one another's pain, but then we move on. We expect each other to hire experts for the complicated stuff, and then report back with the summary. That might sound cold or callous, but it's just the reality of life as a middle-aged person, with all the associated pressures and responsibilities. If you're in a different season of life, your reality might vary. But I've found that in most cases, what adult friends really need is a giggle. We all have so many challenges in our professional and family lives that we tend to seek lightheartedness from our friends. Let's be honest and get real, and then temper our expectations.

SUMMARY

Society uses homophobia to oppress gay men through fear and isolation, to steal our money and our relationships, to eradicate us by misery, and erase our history. The harm is the point. Seen in that light, gay friendship is a radical and revolutionary act of love. It is a political statement of hope and survival. But the unfortunate reality is that many of us internalized this bigotry along the way. Some of us never learned the requisite skills to be a friend, much less find and attract one. But don't despair. These skills can be learned and mastered. The single most important one is the shedding of all the negative love patterns that hold you back and keep you lonely. If you can learn to be your true self, and shine your radiance brightly, people will flock to share your friendship.

The lists of behaviors necessary to fully support our loved ones can seem overwhelming. This is not surprising when you consider that we are fighting centuries of institution-alized bigotry on a number of fronts. It all boils down to otherism: seeing people as different from ourselves, and then punishing them as a way to improve our own socioeco-nomic standing. This bigotry won't just evaporate overnight or on its own, nor will it be easy to manually dismantle. It will take all of our best efforts and require all our partici-pation. But that's what true friendship is about: the lifting up of our loved ones, so that we might know mutual joy and freedom, and celebrate life together, as equals, walking side-by-side.

CHAPTER 8

SEX

Of all that I have endured, by far the worst type of abuse has been neglect. Moving through the world unjoined and unloved is a cruel paradox when you're desperately seeking attention, while also cowering like a house cat under the bed. The result is a life unseen and unwritten, a soul in waiting. I was longing for love's tender mercies. The sweet sense of feeling both seen and sought, of others carving out a space in their lives with my name on it. A steady togetherness that transcends vicissitudes, the confidence and continuity that comes with belonging to a world and a people. And I know I'm not the only one.

Most of us gay men could use more love in our lives. A simple space in this world where we might breathe free. Even those of us with full adult agency sometimes grapple with the residual sexual shame of our childhoods. We wrestle with our internalized messages of bigotry, first foisted on us by society, then amplified by our families, and finally embraced by our darker natures. We wonder why we feel so battered and bruised, exhausted from the struggle, paralyzed by the fear, afraid to ask for what we really want or need. And there are precious few more fundamental human needs than sexual fulfillment. So when they attack us for our sexual behavior, what they are attacking is our humanness.

GETTING REAL ABOUT HOMOPHOBIA

We must start by acknowledging that homophobia is actually a form of sexual abuse. Sex is the focus of their hate, so often the sex act is all straight people see when they look at us, rather than fully realized individuals moving through the same world as everyone else, wanting to love and be loved. When they instill a deep-seeded shame in us—a shame they explicitly link to our sexual orientation— it should not then be surprising that the results are sexual in nature. We can draw a clear line here. When people in power stigmatize our attractions, we either act out or act in on that hate. When they fear or fetishize our entire range of sexual expression, we might internalize those messages. This allows them to distort our behavior and alter our capacity to love. Because that was the entire point. They meant to obliterate us, steal our money, and drain our power. Sex was just the excuse.

Many gay men experienced a delayed emotional adolescence. The denial of society's standard rites of passage in some cases stunted our emotional growth and maturity, and the results were often disastrous. This theft prevented the creation of those memories that would have formed our sense of self. It denied us the opportunity for the regular, low-stakes practice of relationship-building. We never got the chance to invest in a love separate from our families, as we prepared to jump into the adult world. Instead, we were left with a void: missing pieces where our individuality would have gone. And many of those missing pieces were sexual in nature.

When many straight boys were first dipping their toes into the pond of life, most gay boys were too busy hiding their true selves, trying not to get killed. Here are a few contrasting milestones in the lives of some straight and gay boys:

- **First Crush:** some straight boys relish their first crushes on girls, while some gay boys hide in shame, having no clue or context for their new and frightening attraction to other boys.
- **Sexual Sharing:** some straight boys start share their sexual urges about girls with their friends, while some gay boys are too afraid to share their homosexual urges.
- **First Dates:** some straight boys start dating girls in the real world, while some gay boys immerse themselves in homosexual fantasy, since it is unsafe for them to date boys in public.
- **First Kiss:** some straight boys share their first kiss with a girl and feel excited about it, while some gay boys share their first kiss with a girl and feel afraid or ashamed about it, or with a boy and risk rejection or violence.
- **Social Functions:** some straight boys take girls to various social functions (homecoming dances, the prom, etc.), while some gay boys panic and take girls to these events, or stay at home alone, missing out on all these experiences.
- **Sexual Exploration:** some straight boys have their first sexual experience with a girl and fall in love, while some gay boys have their first sexual experience with a girl

and feel lonely or afraid, or with a boy and risk rejection or violence.

It is easy to see the consequences of bias, bigotry, and negative messages towards gay youth, as reflected in the sexual development milestones of many Western cultures. Over the years, the accumulation of these experiences can be both debilitating and disempowering. Some of us don't even reclaim these rites until our mid-twenties or thirties, or much later still. By this time, much of the harm has already taken its toll. The physical, mental, and emotional consequences of our behavior can be drastic and dire.

One of the most common ways we express our internalized sexual shame as gay men is as a crippling fear of intimacy. It used to be illegal for us to congregate, much less show affection. As children, we were steeped in negative messages about our love's lack of worth; this prevents us from sharing physical affection as adults. We might fear holding hands in public, even when it is ostensibly safe and legal. We might refrain from kissing other men, even in the privacy of our own homes. We might scuttle potential relationships as soon as love or commitment enters the picture, even when we really just long to be joined. Perhaps on some level we might prefer pornography to people, even if deep down we want to be seen and known by other men. Maybe we're unduly passive and afraid to ask for what we really want, even when we have full agency. Maybe we are so consumed with self-hate and fear that we suffer from sexual anorexia. There are numerous ways in which we might express our fears of intimacy; many of them go unchecked for years, becoming patterns of negative love or cycles of isolation.

GETTING REAL ABOUT PORNOGRAPHY

Gay youth often grow up culturally alone, without direct access to knowledge or community. This isolation was further compounded for many of us who came of age before the advent of the internet, when access to information or community was spotty at best and downright dangerous at worst. In the absence of sexual mentors and role models, some of us turn to pornography as a lifeline: an educational tool, a method for connection, and a gateway to healthy fantasy. In this regard, access to the internet (and the concomitant proliferation of porn) has been a game changer for many gay youths. They no longer need feel quite so alone. They have a wealth of information on a variety of healthy sex practices. Information that can help them play, learn, and discover, and even save their lives.

Now that the internet is in its third decade, many of us have had a chance to experience its dark side and unintended consequences. From echo chambers to cancel culture, it is clear that this technology is not the utopia for which some of us had hoped. While it's true that we now have access to more online communities and information than ever before, it's also true that, if left unchecked, our patterns of negative love can rear their ugly heads. Many of us reflexively turn to our smart phones whenever we feel bored or uncomfortable. As a result, we are losing the ability for stillness and sustained reflection. We immerse ourselves in unhealthy fantasies in the sexual sphere, at the expense of human connection.

If as children we were tormented and abused by the objects of our desire, as adults these adverse experiences might distort our sense of sexual self-esteem. They can even cause us to conflate pain with pleasure. Over time, we might recreate these childhood experiences in fantasy or our choices in pornography. Both act as a means for us to manifest some sort of power, a mode over which we hold sole dominion. This strategy can be a healthy and effective stopgap, until we find the capacity for real healing and transformation. But in some cases, it backfires. Eventually we might ritualize these fantasies as we continue to chase the high. These rituals can grow into fetishes, as our need for darker and more intense pornography grows more desperate. Eventually, regular human contact no longer fulfills us, and we end up feeling even more powerless and alone.

Sexual fantasies are healthy and wonderful, so long as they don't derail the rest of our lives. If we find ourselves engaging with pornography for hours a day, it's time to take stock. What is it really costing us, not just in terms of cash, but opportunity, and emotional resilience? And what is the accumulated toll? Perhaps we are using pornography to avoid other issues or feelings in our lives. Maybe it keeps us in our comfort zone. If we were to monitor the type of pornography we consume over the course of a few weeks or months, we might notice some patterns. Maybe it's escalating in quality and quantity. Maybe the characters in the pornography we consume are experiencing increasing distress or even abuse. Or maybe we're keeping secrets about our use of pornography.

If we find ourselves looking at increasingly lurid images of men in extreme circumstances, we might be engaged in some sort of personal shame cycle. If that idea resonates, it might be a great time to get curious and do some inquiry. What are we getting out of this behavior? How do we feel before, during, and after the experience? This information will help us get empowered and ask some important questions. If we feel powerless over pornography, there are all sorts of programs available to help us. As always, I recommend contacting a paid mental health professional to help you review the various underlying issues and the wide array of available options. In the end, you are your own best advocate and must do what's right for you.

GETTING REAL ABOUT CONSENT

As we venture out to share sexual relationships with others, we will invariably encounter issues of consent. Men of all sexual orientations are sharing more of their sexual abuse stories than ever before, which is critical if we're truly going to heal. Their honesty has laid bare some of the struggles and transgressions which many of us have endured. Unfortunately, with our frequent focus on freedom and play, sometimes consent gets lost in our community. Somewhere along the way, we gay men learned how to dial up the allure, but not necessarily how to ensure our partners are on the same page. Maybe we just assume everyone is okay, and hope for the best. Maybe we fear that checking in on their well-being will kill the mood. Or maybe we fear the truth. But whatever our apprehension, continuous consent can enhance our sexual experience, if incorporated with confidence, caring, and fun.

But consent alone is not enough. For most of us, there's nothing less sexy than feeling disregarded. Disregard inhibits intimacy, keeps us stuck in our comfort zones, and reduces us to mere roles. Empathy brings us closer together and creates space for us to be ourselves. It allows us to be seen, risks everything, and thus intensifies the thrill. In this setting, empathy is not any one thing. It's the artful mixture of words and touch that communicates what we want, receives and respects our partners' needs, establishes ground rules, and sets the stage for escalating arousal. During healthy sex, we demonstrate empathy and consent continuously, throughout the process of seduction, the sexual act itself, as well as the aftercare. This continuity of experience over time builds trust, which allows us to deepen our pleasure and exploration, without sacrificing our essence, health, or wellness.

Sexual consent alone is actually a pretty low bar when you think about it. Consent says nothing about our mutual health or wellness. Many of us consent to behavior in the moment that's not truly in our best interests, or even what we really want. Agreeing to sexual behavior that we don't really want can come from a variety of past experiences, ranging from the seemingly unrelated to the truly traumatic. In some cases, our consent is impaired or uninformed. Maybe we've had too much to drink. Or perhaps we don't have all the information we need to make a healthy choice. Our consent can also become tainted by the consequences of our past experiences. Some of us have an irrational and codependent fear of losing the love of a friend or partner. Others experience a mental shutting down when confronted with sexual violence reminiscent of prior trauma.

Once instilled in our bodies, this pattern can present as any number of seemingly benign behaviors. Perhaps your partner asks you to act in ways that make you feel uncomfortable, yet you comply out of fear. Or maybe you're the one pushing your partner further and further, without first having open and honest discussions. Perhaps you push your partner away, opting for isolation. Or maybe you find secret consolation in the arms of others. The consequences of our behavior can be readily apparent to many who know us; in others they go hidden for years. But what remains consistent is an absence of intimacy, and the sense that we are slowly hollowing out our insides. We are stuck in some unseen cycle, and even though our bodies are naked, we are missing the insight of tender honesty and the strength of loving kindness.

GETTING REAL ABOUT SEX WITH STRAIGHT GUYS

So many of us get hung up on straight guys. And it's no wonder, since our media is saturated with them. We are born into a world that has monetized masculinity, and taught us to idolize a specific set of behaviors. But these masculine norms are in reality pretty repugnant: the unapologetic objectification and pursuit of women, the avoidance of emotional availability and expression, the insatiable accumulation of power and wealth, and the list goes on. There are human beings on the other side of these media portrayals, and what we do to men in this society is inexcusable.

Some of us idolize straight men out of some strange mix of envy and hate. On the one hand, they represent everything we have ever wanted to be, and in some cases never were. Yet on the other hand, we have some deep-seated need to reclaim our power. To hit back at those that tormented us, such that we might experience what it's like to feel strong and safe. If you've gone your entire life never knowing what it feels like to move through the world without fear, the combination of safety and strength can be both intoxicating and self-destructive.

There is absolutely nothing wrong with a sexual attraction to men, even if those men are straight. When I see a beautiful man, it fills my heart with joy and my body with longing. And I'm not going to pray about it. But when fantasies prevent us from experiencing reciprocal emotional and physical intimacy, we have a problem. If we think straight men are better than gay men, we have a problem. If we only have sex with straight men, we have a problem. If we filter effeminate men from our lives, we have a problem. If we think someone is "too gay," we have a problem. If our preferences become prejudices, we have a problem.

In fact, our preferences themselves are culturally constituted. Left unexamined, these preferences might start to control us. Before we know it, years go by while we get lonelier and lonelier. We chase our fantasies in lieu of love, shoving intimacy and connectedness to the side. But if we broaden our view and examine the preferences that drive our behaviors, the resulting awareness can actually help break the spell. It can snap us back into reality, such that we might experience more intimacy and know more love. We can then build real relationships, based on heartfelt connections and shared energy, as we set down our daydreams, and cast out our internalized homophobia.

The words we use to describe our culture and orientations are dynamic. And to make matters more complicated, nature does not respect our categorizations. That means it can feel frustrating to describe ourselves—to align what we feel on the inside with what we present on the outside—

especially for those who might be new to this language, or not yet have context for this journey. Sometimes labels feel empowering. Other times they feel limiting. I encourage you to use them or set them down pragmatically, based on how you feel or what you need.

Here's how I think about these categories:

GENDER

- **Sex:** the categories (male, female, intersex, etc.) into which we categorize living things, primarily based on reproductive functions.
- **Gender Orientation:** a range of *identities* (man, woman, nonbinary, genderqueer, etc.) based on some combination of sex, appearance, and cultural norms. These identities exist on a spectrum, and can either be fluid or fixed.
- **Gender Expression:** a range of *behaviors* (masculine, feminine, etc.) based on some combination of sex, appearance, and cultural norms. These behaviors exist on a spectrum, and can either be fluid or fixed.
- **Transgender:** a person whose identity does not correspond with the sex assigned at their birth. Trans men are men. Trans women are women. They can be gay or straight, with a range of sexual orientations, attractions, and experiences. This orientation can either be fluid or fixed. They can be gay or straight, with a range of sexual orientations, attractions, and experiences.
- **Non-binary (also known as "Gender Queer"):** a person who does not identify as a man or a woman, but as somewhere on the spectrum and potentially outside the range of the gender binary. Sometimes they asso-

ciate with trans people, since their identity does not correspond with the sex assigned at their birth. This orientation can either be fluid or fixed. They can be gay or straight, with a range of sexual orientations, attractions, and experiences.

- **Non-gendered (also known as "agender" or "post-gendered"):** a person who identifies as having no gender at all. Sometimes they associate with trans people, since their identity does not correspond with the sex assigned at their birth. This orientation can either be fluid or fixed. They can be gay or straight, with a range of sexual orientations, attractions, and experiences.
- **Cisgender:** a person whose identity corresponds with their sex assigned at birth. They can be gay or straight, with a range of sexual orientations, attractions, and experiences.

SEXUAL ORIENTATION

- **Homosexual:** an attraction or experience to/with people of the same sex. When viewed as an orientation, it exists on a spectrum, and can either be fluid or fixed.
- **Bisexual:** an attraction or experience to/with people of either sex. When viewed as an orientation, it exists on a spectrum, and can either be fluid or fixed.
- **Pansexual:** an attraction or experience to/with people of any sex (extending beyond the gender binary). When viewed as an orientation, it exists on a spectrum, and can either be fluid or fixed.
- **Asexual:** a fixed lack of sexual attraction to/with people of any sex. Asexuality does not necessarily obviate romantic attraction, relationships, or even sexual coupling.

- **Heterosexual:** an attraction or experience to/with people of the opposite sex. When viewed as an orientation, it exists on a spectrum, and can either be fluid or fixed.

SEXUAL CULTURE

- **Lesbian:** a culture comprised primarily of homosexual, bisexual, pansexual, and asexual women (including trans).
- **Gay:** a culture comprised primarily of homosexual, bisexual, pansexual, and asexual people (of all gender orientations, including trans) with more of a focus on those *inside* mainstream gender expression norms.
- **Queer:** a culture comprised primarily of homosexual, bisexual, pansexual, and asexual people (of all gender orientations, including trans) with more of a focus on those *outside* mainstream gender expression norms.
- **Straight:** a culture comprised primarily of heterosexual people (of all gender orientations, including trans), with a focus on those *inside* mainstream norms regarding gender expression.

Nature is delightfully messy, and people are beautifully complex. We defy categorization. Some men have penises. Some don't. Some men have both penises and vaginas. Some have neither. Body parts do not denote gender. It's what's inside that counts.

So what does it mean for a man to have sex with a straight guy? If you accept my definitions, "straight" is just a sexual culture based on sexual orientation. A "guy" is just someone who identifies as male. So what's the big deal? What are we really attracted to? Is it his penis? His body hair? His muscles? The way he walks or talks? The most important sexual organ is the brain; the stories we create about sexual orientations, sexual cultures, and gender exist primarily in our heads. When we recognize that fact, we can release ourselves from their grip and set ourselves free. We can relax and have fun, share the energy, and enjoy the ride.

GETTING REAL ABOUT SAFER SEX

There are few guarantees in this life, but that should not stop us from living. When it comes to sex, if we get educated and informed, we can dramatically reduce the odds of harming our bodies or contracting a Sexually Transmitted Infection (STI). Many of us stay silent about our love lives, out of some combination of fear and shame. But that silence can kill us, as the old saying goes. It makes us reliant on gossip and misinformation, in lieu of facts. And it prevents us from sharing knowledge with our loved ones and our healthcare providers.

There are many types of STIs we are all at risk of contracting. But we need not live in fear. Taking charge of our physical health is ultimately a loving act for our partners, and their partners, and their partners. The ripple effects are profound. HIV is a virus—nothing more, nothing less. It is not indicative of the cleanliness of your body or the rectitude of your morality. Unlike people, HIV does not discriminate. Any of us can contract it. But for many of us who grew up during the height of deaths due to AIDS, we no longer need live with those levels of fear. Nowadays those of us with access to the appropriate treatments need not die the exotic, terrifying deaths of our brothers.

Most strains of HIV result in manageable infections, and when treated appropriately, most people who contract HIV can live long, healthy, and full lives. In fact, many come to a place where their viral loads are undetectable, which means they are completely incapable of transmitting the virus to anybody. These days many sero-discordant couples (a couple where one member is HIV+ and the other is HIV-) choose not to use condoms. This poses no negative impact on their health, so long as the HIV+ member is undetectable. If you find yourself commenting on someone else's HIV status, it's time to take stock. If you have your dating apps set to filter out HIV+ men, it's time to take a long, hard look in the mirror.

Currently, HIV prevention drugs only stop the transmission of HIV. So even if you use a drug like PrEP as directed, you might still contract syphilis, herpes, or any other STI. Abstinence is the only foolproof way to avoid infection. However, refraining from sexual contact for extended periods of time can have profound consequences on your mental and physical health. Straight society has also used abstinence education for centuries as the vehicle for their misogyny and homophobia. My hope is that you think carefully about any periods of abstinence. Talk candidly with your healthcare providers and your loved ones to ensure you are not simply acting out of fear. This of course assumes you do not identify as asexual. If your sexual orientation falls somewhere on the Ace spectrum, then prolonged periods of abstinence might be your norm. In these cases, it is still a great idea to consult with your healthcare provider to discuss any potentially adverse and unintended consequences on your health.

For those not on the Ace spectrum, condoms are the safest

way to prevent the transmission of STIs, while still maintaining a healthy and vibrant sex life. When used correctly, condoms are incredibly effective. Yet a shocking number of people still do not know how to correctly size, fit, lubricate, or utilize a condom. I encourage you to utilize the wealth of available materials and to speak to your healthcare professional, so you can prevent any STI transmissions due to incorrect condom usage.

Many men still loathe condoms because they fear it dampens the mood or dulls their sensations. This does not have to be the case. But even so, the cost-benefit analysis is clear. A course of STI medications is probably much less desirable for the vast majority of us than a few hours of slightly increased pleasure. The key is that we think through these issues prior to the moment of sexual contact—when our resistance grows weak, and we are most likely to throw our boundaries out the window. The greater clarity we have going into a situation, the more likely we will be able to take care of ourselves and our partners. This is a biological issue, not a moral one. So by all means, play. Have fun. But let's get real about the risks and the underlying science.

Whether or not you use a condom, there are other behaviors that can help lessen the risk of STI transmission. Lately it has become vogue for men to use an anal douche prior to bottoming. But the problem is that, if done improperly, this behavior can actually increase STI transmission. The wrong kind of douche (by shape) or the wrong kind of solution (such as tap water), can disrupt the environment of the anus—stripping away the oils, hairs, and skin which are meant to protect us. The best thing you can do is speak to a qualified medical professional. They need not be gay, but should understand the mechanics of anal sex, and thus have access to the latest information, with none of the associated stigma. If you sense bias in your doctor, it might be time to either challenge that bias or get a new doctor. You need not suffer in silence.

GETTING REAL ABOUT MONOGAMY

Monogamy might be a cultural norm in many modern-day societies, but it is not intrinsically part of our human design. One of the most thrilling aspects of gay culture is our liberation from any life scripts, involving love and relationships. The set of rules that bind straight society into rigid roles and behaviors don't have to dictate our lives. As gay men, much of straight society has ignored us, shunned us, and cast us aside. But the upside to that bigotry is we have the space to create the lives we want, including our love lives.

Some of us will gladly choose marriage (or our closest legal proximity) as our ultimate expression of love and commitment. And that's beautiful. Others of us will choose to live single lives, floating from one relationship to the next. And that's also beautiful. And still others of us will form romantic bonds with more than one person, potentially even groups of people. And that's equally beautiful. The convergence of love, honesty, consent, and fun requires no set number. Even if our love lives defy description, that's okay, just as long as love is still present.

If monogamy is the practice of having one sexual relationship at a time, then polygamy (or more commonly, "polyamory") is just the opposite: the practice of having more than one sexual relationship at a time. Neither need carry any moral weight. We get to choose only our own morals, and need not subscribe to anyone else's. I've always found it curious why some gay men are so threatened by the love lives of our brothers. Homophobia I get. That's just about the theft of money and power. But why are some of us afraid of polyamory? Are we seeking proximal power by selecting morals that appear more palatable to the conventional tastes of straight society? Could it be that some small part of us hopes if our relationships look more similar to theirs, then our associated rights are less likely to be stripped away? Whatever the case, there is never a good day for prejudice or discrimination. Gentle curiosity and loving kindness are much saner responses. The goal of diversity is not to iron out our differences, but to delight in them and allow those differences to strengthen us as they enrich our lives.

Of course the opposite is also true: monogamy can be both heteronormative and *still* right for you. It doesn't make you boring or conventional as a gay man to desire marriage or some sort of monogamous partnership. The institution might have patriarchal roots, but it can still be valid for you. Your monogamy can look like whatever you wish, and only represents one part of you. We are manifold beings, only partially defined by our relationships, and even our relationships are only partially defined by their structure. So don't let anyone put you in a box out of convenience, or to appease their righteous indignation. Be yourself, stand tall, and walk with pride.

GETTING REAL ABOUT ROMANCE

Commitment need not be the death nail of romance. And

yet, romance often changes with the seasons of our relationships, as well as the seasons of our lives. Our romantic wants and needs in our fifties are unlikely to be identical to what they were in our thirties. The same can be said of a relationship that is relatively new, as compared to one that is decades old. But these changing qualities need not imply reduced quantities of sex and romance. Many people experience an increased sex drive as they age. In many relationships sexual intimacy improves as it matures.

It all starts with our bodies. If we are overweight, we might experience blood flow issues to those parts of our bodies we use during sex, we might experience an undue lethargy in general, or even worse, we might succumb to the shame of our fat-phobic society. Likewise if we are underweight, we might experience many of the same issues. There is an optimum weight range that will feel right for you, and support you as you create the life of your dreams. One great way to work indirectly on a lackluster sex life is to get curious about your body. What is it telling you? What does it need to function? As we age, our bodies change. Cis men might experience a significant loss of their natural testosterone production as they age, which could impact their sex drive. A simple blood test can help determine your testosterone levels, and then you can work with your healthcare professionals to address the underlying issues.

How do we experience stimulus in our bodies? Have we divorced ourselves from all sensation into a kind of sexual anorexia? Do we breeze past sensuality as we chase or avoid orgasms? Or do we savor every touch and smell, as we bask in the wonder of the world and embody each moment? Orgasm might be the top of the mountain that we climb during sex, but there are numerous other pleasures each step of the way. Do we fully experience those pleasures in our body, or de we bypass them, or even reject them?

The most important sex organ is our brain. What past sexual traumas have we experienced that might impact our love lives today? What stories do we tell ourselves about sex? What do we think about our bodies, and the bodies of our partners? How do we communicate these issues with our partners? Do we cultivate an emotional tension that supports our ongoing lust and longing, or do we require peace at all costs? Do we play with polarity as we cultivate sexual fantasy to stoke the fires of lust, or are we locked into rigid roles that suffocate and smother our desire?

Romance is that mix of love and longing that connects us to our sexual needs. Depending on where you might or might not fall on the Ace spectrum, it involves lust, but also transcends it. For many in relationships, the act of romantic intent precedes and accelerates lust. Sometimes the mood just strikes us, and we reach for our partners with a sense of wild abandon. But in many cases, romance involves planning, empathy, and kindness. This is especially true as we reckon with our middle-aged bodies and navigate our durable relationships, fraught with longstanding feuds and forgiveness. Romance is the bridge that connects us. We set the mood to get in the mood. We wine and dine and date to create and hold space for our beloved, and then we pounce with lust and desire. This is how we date our spouse or significant others, no matter how much water is under the bridge. It is a practice that we do, rather than waiting for love's longing to magically descend upon us. This practice is how we get empowered in our relationships and take charge of our love lives.

There are so many different ways we can evoke desire for and from our partners. The foundation for attraction is authenticity. When we wear masks or play inadvertent roles, our partners can sense our hiding, and are on some level repelled by it. Masks as a form of intentional fantasy and play are one thing, but the secret hiding we do from one another erodes desire. Inevitably, when we regularly encounter a partner's authentic being, a familiarity develops. It is this authenticity which prevents that familiarity from devolving into boredom and complacency. True authenticity is never boring.

Complexity is baked into our human design. When we are embodying our most authentic selves, a certain friction develops with our partners. That friction can manifest as arguments or disagreements in a way that feel threatening to many of us who just seek peace and quiet. But this tension also evokes desire. As we fight, our pulses race and our adrenaline rises. And if we are fighting fair and in the spirit of selfless love, I have found that inevitably we come together again in physical union. If you are on the asexual spectrum, this friction might manifest in a variety of subtler ways, or not at all, which is completely healthy and normal. In these cases, it is critical to find other ways to express love and longing in your relationship, based on your individual wants, needs, and orientation.

Many of us are psychologically hardwired to respond sexually to healthy tension. We feel safe when we encounter it, as if it is a measuring stick for the desire, care, and concern of our partners. That tension helps us feel needed, and being needed can evoke our sexual longing. With this in mind, no longer do we need to trick our partners into sex, or beg for their physical attention. When we manifest our personal authenticity and learn the art of harnessing the inevitable friction, we exude an effortless charisma and can channel those energies in a sexual direction. This is different than sexualizing anger; it's the natural result of hearts that soften in the wake of disagreement. The fighting might be rough, but the making up is so much fun!

Some love and relationship experts advocate sexual polarity as a way to stoke desire with our partners. The idea is that one partner plays the role of the masculine dominate and the other of the feminine submissive. These roles (which can be fluid and different than gender orientation) actually stoke our sexual desire for one another. I have to admit a certain bias against this concept, since it seems to reinforce outdated norms regarding gender expression. Advocates tend to frame this concept in terms of the masculine and the feminine, even as they give lip service to nontraditional gender roles. I offer this theory as something for you to explore, but not an idea to feel constrained or beholden to. You can play with polarity without gendering it, or you may gender it if that resonates with you. Just discuss it candidly with your partners.

GETTING REAL ABOUT SEX ADDICTION

In some cases, we might resort to a quantity or quality of sex that is outside the bounds of what we really want, or is even sustainable by the human body. This can feel as if you're living in a constant state of sexual arousal, forever on the hunt. For decades, straight people have used the stereotypes of unchecked masculinity run amok to keep us single and scared, prevent us from legalizing our relationships, and prevent them from examining their own bigotry. They portrayed us as sexual predators, unfit for the fabric of society. They reduced us to caricatures of lust and longing. Some of us internalized these roles—reacting to them as a mix of perpetrators (sadists) or victims (masochists). Somehow this play became entangled in our personal liberation, until what some of us truly wanted got lost along the way. There's absolutely nothing morally wrong with our fetishes or fantasies, so long as they are safe, consensual, and fun. But there is also an issue of capacity. If our sexual behaviors consume us, then we lose our ability to construct well-rounded lives, and the behaviors outlive their usefulness.

It's healthy to examine the costs of all our behaviors, including sex. How much money a month do we spend on sexual stimulation? Has chasing a sexual high cost us friendships, jobs, injured our reputations, or harmed our bodies? Nobody can answer these questions for us, and we avoid them at our peril. To ignore them is to be at their mercy, and to procrastinate is to roll the dice, hoping that today will be a day of fewer consequences, magically different than the day before. And so it all comes down to personal inquiry—creating the awareness that will help us make those healthy choices that empower us to live our best lives.

In some cases, we have become addicted to sex. Addiction is any compulsive, mood-altering behavior that renders our lives unmanageable. Just about any behavior can be addictive. Sex addiction is the unsustainable use of sexual stimulation and orgasm to avoid our problems or any feelings we deem undesirable. Perhaps we had a rough day at the office, and we opt to hire a sex worker rather than feel our feelings. Maybe we had a fight with our husband, so we decide (in secret) to hook up with a stranger, rather than experience the anguish of our anger. Perhaps we masturbate for hours a day because we're too afraid to get out there and live our own lives.

In and of themselves, these behaviors could lie in any number of places on the spectrum of addiction. Perhaps they are compulsive, because we lack the ability to refrain from them in the short term. Or maybe they are just transitory behaviors that we use to avoid something in the short term. Addiction speaks to the cost and stubbornness of our behaviors and goes beyond mere impulse control. Addiction implies we can't help but cling to our behaviors, even as they destroy us, erode our integrity, gobble up our money, poison our relationships, and rob us of everything we thought we had—until all that's left is chasing a high that proves increasingly elusive.

Only we can name and claim our addictions because only we can truly assess the impact on our lives and the consequences of our behaviors. Nobody can do it for us. Others might intervene to grab our attention and shift our awareness, but we won't truly recover until we admit where we are, embrace the work, and then do the work. Over and over, day by day. In the recovery of addiction, there are no finish lines. The goal is a spiritual transformation such that we might birth a new freedom. But we are forever just one behavior, one poor choice away from repeating our addiction cycle. Addiction recovery requires a soft, lifelong vigilance, such that we might both change our choices and recover the feeling of joy.

SUMMARY

As gay men, it has been so easy for us to slink in the shadows. The penalties of transgressing the expectations of straight society can be severe. For centuries, their most extreme punishments were reserved for the sexual sphere because in their eyes we were only gay when we were engaged in the sex act. The rest of our lives simply didn't count. As a result, sex became symbolic of the ultimate expression of our humanness, when we were both most alive and most vulnerable. But their oppression didn't stop there. To protect themselves from our sex lives, straight people had to fire us from our jobs, deny us housing, end our relationships, and refuse us entry to society at large. One decision led to another, until all they could do was try to pray us altogether out of existence. For there is no sinner without the sin, and the vast majority of human beings cannot exist without sexual fulfillment. Besides, in the end, what would they have us do? Repent and then marry their daughters?

If I could impress just one thing upon you, it would be this: our secrets are killing us. Like the old slogan goes, so it remains—not just in the lingering shadow of AIDS, but in the slow deaths of self-abnegation we experience when we play it small, and in the countless ways our bodies atrophy amidst this epidemic of loneliness. We toughen our hides, as we cut our teeth on each other's flesh. We scramble over the backs of our brothers, desperately seeking higher ground amidst the rising waters of fear. Hungry for home, yet clawing for crumbs, determined to deny it all, if only once, just once, straight people might give us some small nod of approval.

Gay liberation is not about garnering the praise of a homophobic society, or imitating any number of media-driven narratives about "normal" relationships. It isn't the extreme reaction against their strange suburban moral standards, or narrowcasting to facilitate easier family conversations during the holidays. Gay liberation is about the right for us to exist as we are. Right here. Right now. Today. And to thrive—removing the stigma of our orientation; opening doors to a wealth of opportunities; eliminating tax and legal punishments; implementing and protecting equal accommodation to housing, employment, and marriage; and experiencing the full range of our humanity and culture. Nowhere does this idea hit home more for gay men than in our love lives. And the more awareness we can muster, the stronger we will find our voices, as we proudly proclaim who we are, live openly and honestly, stand behind our choices and identities, and boldly embrace those behaviors that serve us, as we revel in our play.

CHAPTER 9

COMMUNITY

Let's face it. The LGBTQIA+ community can seem like a strange and unlikely collection of disparate groups: an uneasy coalition of outcasts, united to fight for similar issues, if not for a single, common cause. Those of us in this community are bound by our bodies, standing for how we love, and struggling to protect those whom we love. Maybe this fragmentation is why it has been so easy for straight society to divide and distract us. Why our community has yet to embrace any unifying leaders or spokespeople. Why so many of us have fought and marched together, yet still felt disjointed. Why we have also sometimes turned our anger inward, on each other.

Maybe the logical result of oppression occurring within a container of social isolation is an apprehension to band together, even with our own allies. When we grow up separate and alone, with no sense of shared culture, fearing, fighting, and rejecting our identity, as well as everyone else's, it is no wonder we have trouble uniting. Perhaps another cost of our journey is a reluctance to trust authority of any kind, even when it comes from within our community. It's not just that as young people we exist outside of straight society, it's that we are also very different from one another. We are creating our cultures from scratch.

When we finally find and embrace our true selves, the first thing many gay men do is seek other gay men. This initial search is often about sex. There is brotherhood in belonging, in dancing together, in laughing together, and in hunting together. But I'm continually surprised by the number of us out gay men who are not friends with other out gay men. So many of us come together just for the sake of coming together, and then separate in sheepishness—fumbling with our phones, slowly shuffling our feet, as we eye our possible exits.

With all that we have faced, it's no wonder we sometimes have trouble trusting our own. But on some level, a community is primarily a group of friends. When you have spent your life experiencing a form of rejection based on your very existence, when you have internalized that rejection as a form of shame and self-hate, and when you have externalized that rejection to run from others like you, friendship can be difficult at best. Consider what happens the next time you initially encounter another openly gay man. Do you sexualize the situation? Do you stammer or hesitate? Do you suddenly go shy? Do you feel unwarranted pressure or expectation? Do you flee? Or are you able to seamlessly slip into a subtle shorthand of shared experiences?

There is something so sweet in these moments, when our solidarity is still burgeoning. If we blow past them with slights, recriminations, or internalized homophobia, something is lost. Sex is often the lure to connectedness among gay men. However, if we always leap into bed without first getting to know each other, we might be missing out. Likewise, if we act out on our internalized homophobia, by dismissing each other through fear, shame, or othering, then we are the ones who are losing. We cannot build community while we sit safely in our isolation. There is no community without communing, which takes trust, established slowly and built over time.

Community invariably involves labeling, the application of our distinctions that help us recognize one another. And like most things among gay men, our labels tend to start with sex. What makes a man gay? Are there different types of gay men? How do we subdivide our community? And just who gets to draw those lines? Does someone else do it for us or to us? Or do we get to self-identify? It can be so easy to label one another, and then get lost in our own Byzantine taxonomy: gay, bi, bear, otter, wolf, etc. But just as empowering as our labels have been for us, so too they might be for others. Consider the pride and joy we felt when we first embraced our own gay identities. Would we deny that experience to anyone else? Would we impose our labels on them? Would we try to place them in our contrived boxes? No, we must be allowed to label ourselves, knowing we will be embraced by our brothers without question.

Categories are valuable. They help us place ourselves in the culture at large, determine where we fit, define who we are, discern why we are the way we are, and inform what's important to us. Categories can be especially helpful in the absence of a culture instilled in us by our family of origin.

But this only works if we select the categories ourselves, in our own time, and based on our own unique understandings. This is the intersection of idiomatic expression and individual experience.

Underneath these labels, we are all human beings, each needing mutual loving kindness to survive and thrive. We have so much in common that our separateness can seem absurd, our labels constricting. It can be tempting to use our labels as a means to draw lines in the sand—to hide behind the coattails of more senior members of our new-found tribe, and close ourselves off from anyone we deem different, unqualified, or unworthy. We must be so careful about our boundaries: ensure that they enhance our lives, rather than constrain them, and support both our differentiation and our inclusion. Our boundaries embody a foundational social paradox: this is me and that is you and we are one.

GETTING REAL ABOUT COMING OUT

If you accept my previous distinction between "gay" (a cultural identity) and "homosexual" (a sexual orientation), then coming out is a prerequisite to membership in the gay community. In fact it's the only qualification. You're gay if you say you're gay. Nobody else gets a vote. No one can deny you membership. But come out you must. Until then, you might experience same-sex attraction, or engage in same-sex behaviors. You might even identify homosexuality as your fixed sexual orientation. But until you are living the life, you are not yet gay, not yet part of the culture. And it's impossible to fully live this life without coming out.

Living as an openly gay man does not mean you live in a

coastal, urban center. It does not mean you have a high-paying job. It does not mean you go to circuit parties. It does not mean you love fashion. It does not mean you cut hair for a living. It does not mean you accentuate your more feminine qualities. It does not mean you sleep with hundreds of new men each year. It does not mean any of the other clichés, tropes, or caricatures that the mass media perpetuates about us. It just means you embrace all of yourself, including your sexual orientation, and that you support the liberation of other gay men and all people in the LGBTQIA+ community.

Some openly gay men live in Middle America, including small towns. Some openly gay men behave in ways that others might consider masculine. Some openly gay men work in blue collar jobs. Some openly gay men remain quite close to their families of origin. Some openly gay men have children. Some openly gay men are monogamous. Some openly gay men love sports. Some openly gay men routinely spend time in the great outdoors. There is no one way to be gay. Being gay cannot be quantified—nobody is "gayer" than anyone else. You either join the community, or you don't. What out gay men have in common is that we live openly and honestly, and that we support one another.

Coming out is rarely a one-time event, and can often be a daily process. Sure, there was the moment when we first came out to our friends and loved ones, and when we tell our coming out stories; that's often what we are referring to. But if we commit to living openly and honestly, we will find ourselves routinely disclosing the realities of our lives to a variety of people: whenever someone assumes we are straight, and we correct them; whenever someone makes a derogatory comment about a fellow member of our community, and we speak our truth; and whenever we resist discriminatory housing or employment practices aimed at our community. If we marry our stories to any of these experiences, they are all different ways of coming out.

Just as coming out is not a singular experience, closeting is not a singular experience. We choose to closet ourselves in many situations over the course of our lives, for all sorts of reasons, usually having to do with personal safety. We fear our safety is at risk if we disclose this truth, and celebrate this part of ourselves. It may be that we came out years (even decades) ago, yet at some point find ourselves in a situation where we yield to fear. We shield ourselves from straight society, and attempt to hide or "pass." Perhaps we fear missing out on a promotion, losing our job, being denied housing, or being physically assaulted. The reality of our world is that sometimes these decisions are righteous. They are sacred, personal choices, about which none of us should apply moral judgments. The most loving thing we can do is welcome one another back into our community with open arms, as they are ready, no questions asked.

GETTING REAL ABOUT OUR RELATIONSHIPS WITH LESBIANS

Too often when we gay men refer to the LGBTQIA+ community, we really just mean gay men. All those other people are afterthoughts. And of course by gay men, we more than likely mean gay, cis men. Or even, white, gay, cis men. Or rather masculine, white, gay, cis men. Okay, able-bodied, masculine, white, gay, cis men. Able-bodied, masculine, white, gay, cis men with big penises. Able-bodied, masculine, white, gay, cis men with big penises and huge sex drives. But not too huge. Or weird. In fact, it's probably best if they're just like us. Or at least those carefully curated versions of ourselves that we save for social media. Diversity creates richness and strength. Bigotry just creates clones—purity at the expense of fidelity.

One unintended consequence of our cloning behavior has been that too many of us gay men have not spent enough time with women, especially lesbians. Sure we might pal around with a few straight women, but that's very different. Our relationships with straight women are mutually advantageous and nonthreatening. They're often based in part on the thrill of uniting male and female energy in a society that says men and women can't be friends. In a strange way, over time, these relationships sometimes inadvertently reaffirm our separateness and aloneness, especially if we allow our gayness to be a role that we play. But at the time, they can feel both safe and edgy. They can seem familiar yet fun, as we unite our worlds and play with the resulting emotional tension.

Friendships between gay men and bisexual or pansexual women seem more common than friendships between gay men and lesbians. Maybe that has something to do with the way straight society places strange parameters on the acceptability of same-sex attraction among women. It's often a desirable (and even fetishized) trait, just so long as in the end the woman ends up with a man, and no gender norms are threatened along the way. Maybe that dynamic has permeated gay culture. But when female same-sex attraction becomes both a sexual orientation and a cultural identity, all of a sudden many gay men seem to have a problem. We find cultivating friendships with lesbians threatening.

The media-driven narrative about our divisions only exacerbates this dynamic. These relationships push us out of our cultural comfort zone. But more troubling is that many gay men carry a strain of misogyny that threatens our relationships with all women. Our biases have formed a wedge in our relatedness, which has only contributed to the need for women-only spaces, as well as a need for lesbian-led movements, to fight for those rights we gay men have ignored. If some lesbians find us to be fickle or flippant, who could blame them? How could they help but roll their eyes at our fetishes of toxic masculinity, our tacit embrace of a sexist popular culture, our mindless worship of male privilege, and our active participation in the racist aspects of our society? It's everything they have fought against for decades.

Maybe our bigotry is born from an innate desire to pursue other men, whether gay or straight. This desire does not just separate us from women, but causes us to curry favor with men on the backs of women's liberation. It too easily joins the misogyny of others, in order to disguise our own secret longings, and inevitably cozies up to those who (even inadvertently) are invested in female oppression. When was the last time any of us openly gay men listened, I mean really listened, to the fear and pain and shame of any woman in our lives? When was the last time we marched with them in solidarity on any issue that does not directly impact us?

As we form a coalition, there are questions which all of us in the community must consider. What do gay men and lesbians share culturally, outside of our same-sex attractions and struggles with homophobia? When and how do we as gay men engage with lesbians on a personal level? If we don't take the time to get to know lesbians as fully realized, complex people, then how can we expect to effectively unite with them in our political struggles? And let's be clear: there is a debt to be paid. Lesbians have been standing with gay men for generations, patiently accommodating our cultural uniquenesses and eccentricities, while keeping their eyes on the larger prize of intersectional liberation. Put plainly, we have not reciprocated nearly enough. How can we not be moved by their leadership and care during the peak period of our deaths in the AIDS epidemic, their bravery at Stonewall, or their fight for marriage equality?

We gay men rarely deserve the lesbians who have loved us and have fought alongside us when we had the means, and for us when we did not. And yet even after all this, somehow the strains of our misogyny run deep. We are not immune. We don't get a free pass just because we too are part of a minority and have known bigotry. Too often we reduce lesbians to caricatures and punchlines. We marvel at their music and make fun of their fashion. In the best of times, our banter might carry the delightful intonations of little brothers, teasing their more mature sisters. But too often it resembles an oppressive discounting and shaming. It's time for us to genuflect, get real, and grow up.

GETTING REAL ABOUT OUR RELATIONSHIPS WITH TRANS PEOPLE

If we gay men have sometimes been derisive and dismissive of lesbians, then we have been downright violent and hostile to trans women. We often act as if we're afraid of incurring the cost associated with congregating with feminine bodies in a male-dominated world. We live in a society where it's okay to dominate and objectify feminine bodies, but not to have or associate with one. Trans women stand at the forefront of feminine oppression, even at the hands of other feminists, but most dangerously and directly at the hands of men—straight men, who would sexualize and kill them. Yet worse still are we gay men who would stand by silently, allowing them to be beaten or murdered—those of us afraid to lose what little respect we have mustered from straight men, for the sake of someone perceived to be so low on life's ladder.

How often have we gay men cast aside trans women in order to avoid recognition or association, in a gruesome guilt by association? How many times have we excluded them from our spaces because we thought they threatened our masculinity, killed the mood, or made us enhanced targets for police action? Perhaps, for some of us, this violence has been a way to reenact our own self-hatred of our more feminine modes of expression. Perhaps some of us are on gender orientation journeys of our own and have weaponized our self-loathing. Perhaps some of us envy their relations with straight men. Or perhaps some of us just carried the same transphobic fears and fascinations of the rest of society. Whatever the reasons, we gay men have truly harmed trans women, and it is time for us to recognize this and atone.

Our relationships with trans men might even be more complicated, given our slow acceptance of the roles body parts and gender play in our sexual relations. When we say we're attracted to men, do we also create space for our attraction to trans men? If not, then why? Being gay means we are men who celebrate our attraction to other men. But what exactly are we attracted to anyway? Muscles? Body hair? Penises? Do we really think that there are no trans men out there who possess these magical features? So what's really at play here? What are we afraid of?

Beyond the realm of sexual attraction, why are we friends with so few trans men? Is it because some of them are straight? And if so, why would their sexual orientation influence our separation? Should we hold straight, trans men equally accountable for our torment and abuse, just because they share the same sexual orientation as straight, cis men? How many of us have ever been abused by a straight, trans man? And if not, what are we afraid of? Issues of our own masculinity? More guilt by association? Or do we just assume we lack common ground, simply by virtue of the differences in our cultural upbringing? We've got to get real about these questions if we are ever going to truly welcome trans men into our brotherhood.

GETTING REAL ABOUT OUR RELATIONSHIPS WITH BISEXUAL MEN

Some men are bisexual. Get over it. Sure, many of us as young, gay men originally came out as bisexual, in an effort to delay the inevitable embrace of our homosexuality, or at least soften the blow of going all the way gay. And many of us have known men who claimed to be bisexual, when they were really just closeted, out for a little something on the side, before heading home to their wives. It's easy to resent their ability to straddle both worlds, code switch seamlessly, and avoid all that we had endured: the fear, the beatings, or the lack of choice in employment and housing. And so we lashed out, telling ourselves that *all* bisexual men must be like this, that *none* of them can be trusted.

I'm sure some bisexual, cis men took advantage of this dynamic, but that's on them. We gay men need to let it go. Because nobody can truly take advantage of us unless we let them. And bisexuality is different than the down low. The fact that some of us might have had some negative experiences with cis men who only claimed to be bisexual does not obviate the existence of a full sexual spectrum. Just because *some* men deceived us, or themselves, does not mean *all* bisexual people are lying. It's unfair to paint all of them with that brush.

Logic dictates that inevitably bisexual people must comprise the largest segment of the LGBTQIA+ community. Some bisexual people are cis, and some are trans. Some bisexual people are men, while others are women. Some have shared sexual experiences with both men and women, some haven't. Some bisexual people have sexual urges for men and women simultaneously, others don't. Some experience equal attraction to both men and women, while others lean more one way or the other. Bisexual people are not intrinsically "in denial" or lying. Bisexual people are not automatically more masculine or feminine than gay or straight people. They are not objects to be feared or fetishized. Like all of us, they are just people on the many spectrums of love and relatedness.

The human heart is deep and mysterious. It scoffs at our delicate sensibilities. What is our sexual orientation if 51 percent of our attraction bends toward one gender? What about 99 percent? Who should dictate how we identify? The answer is easy: no one but us. Nobody can silence or erase us, unless we let them. In some cases, other gay men will feel threatened by our individuality (whatever our identity) and try to reabsorb us into the group. Straight society will certainly try to make us into what we are not, but that experience is so much more painful when it's done by one of our own, someone with whom we hoped we had refuge. The mainstream always takes the path of least resistance, and if left unchecked, it will expediently create caricatures out of each and every one of us. That's why it is so critical we resist, that we stand up and be counted in all our various shapes, sizes, races, genders, expressions, and orientations. So that we leave our mark, and the world must reckon with us.

GETTING REAL ABOUT OUR RELATIONSHIPS WITH QUEER PEOPLE

It seems like most of us gay men actually fear queer people. Straight people have hurled that word at many of us in acts of violence and degradation. The word alone carries more stigma for gay men than any other, save one. But from the fires of gay liberation, some have reclaimed it, and then used it as the basis for a new culture, separate and distinct from gay culture. The distinction between gay culture and queer culture boils down to a nontraditional approach to sexual orientation and gender norms, combined with a rejection of the heteronormative mainstream.

Queer people intrinsically threaten the status quo, which too many of us gay men esteem. Gay men want acceptance, while queer people want a fight. To even call yourself queer is to be vaguely threatening—to reclaim your power by embracing an epithet, and thereby put yourself at risk. On some level, I suspect this is part of the appeal: to stand apart from mass media and our consumer culture, to inhabit a space in implicit yet direct opposition to the mainstream, to inquire into the value of mimicking heteronormative power and relationship structures, and to abandon the transactional nature of traditional relatedness—all working hand-in-hand to form a chain of oppression.

It's no wonder then that those of us gay men who have most wanted to align with straight power structures have been the ones who have most feared queer culture. We have desperately wanted to be part of the mainstream, so have avoided anything and everything outside those stark lines. Some of us have even wanted to pass as straight, so we felt a revulsion to the feminine. We grew attached to sexual jargon like "masculine for masculine" (or "M4M"), "straight-acting," or "no femmes."

Aside from the rampant racial prejudices in our community, I believe that we can trace almost all of our internal hate back to our fear of the feminine: our aversion to feminine bodies and feminine mannerisms, and our desperate need to be seen and accepted by straight men, or at least avoid their wrath. Too many of us long to cling to the masculine and create our very own caste system of hate, built on our bigotry. We have inflicted our prejudices on the world; you need go no further than a dating app to watch them play out on a daily basis. So is it any wonder we fear queer people? Those who seem so strong and self-assured in their separateness? Who refuse to apologize for anything, and represent so much of what we wish we were?

GETTING REAL ABOUT OUR RELATIONSHIPS WITH INTERSEX PEOPLE

The term "intersex" describes people born with a range of sex organs and conditions which mainstream medicine considers atypical. Some intersex people are born with a female appearance, but have internal male-typical anatomy. Other intersex people are born with a male appearance, but have internal female-typical anatomy. And there are still other intersex people born with genitalia that seem ambiguous to those healthcare professionals and family members present at their birth.

For instance, some people born with XX chromosomes might have any of the following:

- A large clitoris, which may even resemble a penis
- Fused labia, perhaps even containing lumps that feel like testes
- Labial folds that resemble a scrotum

Some people born with XY chromosomes might have any of the following:

- A small penis, which may even resemble a clitoris
- A divided scrotum, perhaps even missing one or both testicles
- Undescended testicles

There are a variety of other physical traits that can make it challenging for even the most seasoned healthcare professionals to assign a gender at a child's birth. And this is to say nothing of atypical chromosomal or hormonal conditions, which can further complicate the process.

At the end of the day, "intersex" is a culturally constituted category based on a range of physical and biological features. The physical traits and resulting lived experiences of intersex people are real, even if society has created and contrived the groupings. Body parts vary in size and shape, be they breasts, penises, clitorises, scrotums, labia, or gonads. Even sex chromosomes can vary. And yet, for most of us in the Western world, medical professionals and our parents decide what our gender will be at birth, without our input or consent. This decision is not as cut and dry as many might think, yet it impacts the rest of our lives.

So why do parents participate in this outdated practice? Why do healthcare professionals or government officials require a choice? Who has the authority to decide how small a baby's penis has to be before we call it a clitoris? How large does a baby's clitoris have to be before it qualifies as a penis? And why does the size of the organ so often dictate the designation? In modern society, what does male even mean? How about female? What combination of body parts is required to count as intersex? Prenatal exposure to hormones? Mix of testicular and vaginal tissue? How should we gender a person with XXY chromosomes, mosaic genetics, or any other atypical chromosomal traits? What about atypical hormonal traits, like androgen insensitivity? And what qualifies us to make this decision? Who assesses the outcome or the correctness of the decision? And who sets those criteria, as well as the consistency and effectiveness of their application?

What is gender, other than a social construct? What can gender orientations predict about our aptitudes or affinities? Are gender orientations fluid, fixed, or both, at various points in our lives? Can people have multiple genders, or no gender at all? Once you get curious about gender, the whole system seems built on a house of cards; you start to wonder what it's all about in the first place. Historically, gender assignment has been about patrimony, power, and money. But in modern society, why is gender still such a powerful construct? Seen in this light, it can all seem a little arbitrary and facile for so sacred a choice with such steep consequences.

GETTING REAL ABOUT OUR RELATIONSHIPS WITH ASEXUAL PEOPLE

The term "asexual" refers to a sexual orientation that describes people who experience little to no sexual desire. Asexuality is different than celibacy, which is a sustained period of sexual abstinence. Nor is asexuality an issue of low libido: a low sex drive resulting from a variety of physical, psychological, or emotional issues. Asexuality is neither a gender orientation, nor a choice. It is not the result of trauma, nor a hormone imbalance.

Asexuality is a sexual orientation, like homosexuality or heterosexuality. It is not about the presence or absence of orgasm. It is about deep feelings, rather than simple behavior. Like all other sexual orientations, asexuality falls on a spectrum. Some asexual people have sex, and others don't. Some asexual people masturbate, and others don't. Some asexual people have romantic desire, and others don't. Some asexual people identify as straight, while others identify as gay, or queer. Some asexual people identify as cisgendered, while others identify as transgendered.

When asexual people have romantic feelings for someone of the same gender orientation, they might refer to themselves as "homoromantic," which is yet another way of describing an orientation on the spectrum. This orientation does not preclude their asexuality. It's just a further descriptor, indicating that the objects of their romantic attractions are generally of the same gender orientation, even if that attraction is rarely sexual. Likewise, the term "heteroromantic" refers to asexual people who have romantic feelings for someone of the opposite gender orientation. "Biromantic" refers to asexual people who have romantic feelings for someone of either gender orientation; "panromantic" refers to asexual people who have romantic feelings for someone of any gender orientation.

When someone discloses their asexuality to us, they deserve the same love and respect as anyone—the same care and concern we expected when we came out of our closets. When someone reveals their deepest truths, the most loving thing we can do is listen. When it's our turn to speak, what's important is our blessing and affirmation, rather than our opinion. They are seeking an acknowledgment of our shared love and experiences, and a reassurance that our love will not only continue, but be enhanced by this news and increased intimacy. They want us to acknowledge that the world is better off with them in it, living openly and proud.

GETTING REAL ABOUT THE REST OF US

There are many other orientations and identities that we invite and accept into our community, as designated by the "+" in "LGBTQIA+." All who commit to love and support one another are welcome. The categorization of people is a dangerous game. We are well-advised to use these labels as platforms for our own self-empowerment, lest they unwittingly become mere means to divide ourselves further. Each of our groups can be increasingly distilled by the nuances of our bodies or beliefs, until we are standing alone, the sole result of our own purity tests, micro-labeled in the extreme. It requires a combination of courage, discernment, and pragmatism to create and leverage our categories, while balancing our individuality with our community.

It's reductive to collapse other identities in our community into the "+" symbol. And yet, we have struggled to find that one magic label that includes all of us, while being logical and intuitive for society at large. When does a behavior become a preference? When does a preference become a pattern? When does a pattern become an orientation? Is there a hierarchical relationship between these categories? Do they empower or imprison us? How can we leverage labels to better serve each other, as well as society at large? And just who gets to decide all this?

Some of us experience fixed and enduring patterns of sexual attraction or non-attraction. It seems logical to group these patterns as orientations, as opposed to fleeting desires, preferences, or fantasies. But for others, they are not quite as fixed. They might be more fluid, and shift over time, or they might be completely fluid all of the time. How do we label ourselves in these situations? The truth is we just don't yet have the language to label every combination and permutation of attraction. As a community, we are still formulating our terminology, not in the name of taxonomy, but in self-actualization.

As marginalized people in an oppressive society, the better we know ourselves, the easier it is to live openly and honestly. The less apologetic we will be about our true natures. Self-awareness stokes pride. We are social creatures who long to know how we fit in. The hard-fought, clarifying personal growth to mine our souls and extract our essences will lead us to the labels we can use to educate our loved ones. Then we can succinctly disclose our oneness: I am me and you are you. Here is how we are different, and here is how we are alike. I am the same me I have always been, and you are the same you I have always known. But now we have some new words to describe each other, so that we might celebrate our differences and delight in our diversity.

GETTING REAL ABOUT OUR STRAIGHT ALLIES

Straight people are not our enemy. In fact, we currently have more straight allies than at any other time in modern history. It's true that we have suffered centuries of persecution at the hands of straight people, and that bigotry has enslaved them. But the straight community is no more monolithic than the gay community. If we paint all straight people with the same brush, we risk our own liberation. In order for us to integrate into society, we must embrace its pluralism. Straight culture will not disappear in the near term, but it is evolving, just like all cultures. It behooves us to honor that evolution. Not only is it morally the right thing to do, but it is in our best interests.

The straight community currently holds most of the cards. There are precious few openly LGBTQIA+ elected officials in the world. Sure, we have garnered some power through the mass media and the struggles of our ancestors. But we will only win further civil rights by both holding the straight community accountable and honoring our allies. So let's give credit where credit is due, as we continue the fight. That fight looks like overturning any and all existing structural bigotry and anti-LGBTQIA+ laws. It looks like enacting supportive legislation at every level of government. It looks like erasing any and all discriminatory practices in all organizations and businesses, but most particularly in government agencies and institutions. It does not look like calling people names, fomenting hate, yielding to our prejudices, or engaging in our own bigotry.

We deserve better, and we will only get better by rising above that which we have endured. I see no harm however in radical honesty, speaking truth to power, or exposing hypocrisy. However, the "outing" of others in our bigoted society is tantamount to a form of violence; we should reserve it for the most extreme situations. When people in positions of power explicitly use that power to harm our community, while simultaneously engaging our community in secret sex, I believe shining the light on this hypocrisy can save lives. But we would be wise to slow down, seek counsel, and consider the potential unintended outcomes prior to exposing this hypocrisy. If we lob hand grenades over the fence in an act of rage, we risk all the positive change and work of our ancestors, as well as turning into what we once feared.

SUMMARY

Here is my most searing truth: I fear that the light shining through the shards of my brokenness is merely made up of the harsh shafts of self-indulgence, rather than the warm glow of atonement. I worry that the whole of this introspection is less than the sum of its parts. I've spent so much time lost in thought, hiding in the hedges of my mind. And while I fear it's foolish to find meaning in any struggle, I choose to believe in the dignity of discernment. I believe there is no loneliness without love and longing; that we have not abandoned togetherness when our souls yearn to be joined. By singing songs of our self-awareness, we counterstrike our soul's slack and sleeping senses. By preparing ourselves to be known and loved, we carve space in this world to exist and be joined in our grand diversity.

It's easy to reduce the various categories and labels of our community to a game of semantics or "what about-ism." As a layperson, it can all feel so overwhelming. Think how challenging it is for us gay people to keep current with all the various identities and orientations, to remember the myriad nicknames, slang, and jargon, and to abide by the rules. Now just imagine you're straight, and have never thought in these terms. You want to love us, but you're afraid to say the wrong thing. You're worried you'll offend someone, or look stupid. Can we really not empathize with these lovely souls who are so new to engaging our community? Do we truly lack the generosity of spirit to extend a loving hand and invite them in, to forgive their transgressions, and embrace their diversity?

There are those out there who wonder why we even mention our sexualities, much less march. And yet we learned long ago that our silence made us complicit in our own oppression. Our labels are important because real people and real lives are at stake. We must shout these labels from the rooftops to mark our place in the world and plow a path for those who will one day walk it yet. Because, as the old saying goes, you have to see it to be it. In doing so, we also acknowledge the paradox: that while it's critical to broadcast our labels in a heteronormative world, they can never hope to fully encapsulate our complex identities, much less define our community. It's confusing because people are confusing; we confound logic and defy description. Therefore there can be only one answer: we are each of us who we say we are, no questions asked and no explanation required. And it's all beautiful.

CHAPTER 10

SERVICE WORK

There was a time not so long ago when nobody believed in me. When I held a vision of what my life might be, but many of my loved ones could not yet see it, or share in it. They only knew the person I had been, and could not envision who I might one day become. They looked at me with blank eyes as I shared my potential, yawned when I described my mission, and fidgeted when I framed the arc of my life. There is little so lonely as not being joined in your dreams. So I held my light, cupped in my palms like a firefly, desperate to dazzle, but only just yet glowing.

The greatest service we can do for this world is to live our lives to the fullest: embody every ounce of our essence and our values to manifest our mission; bring forth that combination of talent, skill, and experience that is unique to us; and use it to the hilt. When it comes to service work, false modesty helps no one. This is not the time to demure and hide behind the coattails of others. I encourage you to step into the spotlight and sing your song, such that everyone can hear it, even in the back of the hall.

I first found this light years ago, with my then partner at a 12 Step retreat for sex addicts and their spouses. For some reason, they asked me to lead a session about healthy sex, of all things. They wanted me to share my experience, strength, and hope about a topic that was still so new and mysterious to me. But in those days when asked to serve, I always said yes. So I agreed, even though I had no idea what I was doing, and no idea what to expect. I just knew that I had this light, and that I had to share it.

I can still see it all so clearly, as if that past moment is preserved in the living present:

> I walk to the whiteboard and look over my shoulder: "So what do you want to talk about?" I ask the guys, half-joking.

> We are gathered together in a tattered church basement, yet they sit huddled around me, as if waiting for some kind of halftime speech: something to buck them up and send them off, back into the world that has rejected them, so they might resume their fight.

> There is a desperation in their big bodies, as they look up at me. They are both angry and seeking consolation. These sex addicts, about whom I previously might have made a snide remark, now somehow seem both imposing and tender.

> A few of them fidget, sensing I have nothing prepared, almost feeling sorry for me.

Someone shouts: "Just tell us a story!" Others look at the floor and bite their nails, wondering when they can leave.

"Sure, but what do you really want to know?" I respond, hoping for a hook.

No dice.

I turn back to the whiteboard, and jot down a few discussion prompts. The guys warm to me slightly, and offer some suggestions. I add their ideas, and sense a subtle shift in power, as if I'm the one now holding them.

But they have not yet noticed the change. They titter anxiously, eager to move on, assuming my defeat but not yet wanting to be too cruel. That will come later.

Suddenly I turn to face them.

I speak forcefully and my words are electric. Immediately they are rapt, as if nobody has ever talked like this to them before, treated these big, burly men like little boys—boys who might yet be made whole, who could still inherit a past that might have been, had something gone just a little differently.

I have never seen faces like this, almost like dolls: mouths empty as saucers, eyes wide with surprise. Some men bend forward, clutching at their knees. Others rock in their chairs.

I don't have a clue what I'm saying, what I have summoned, brought forth. I just know that it's brilliant, that for this one hour in time, something seizes me, and I am luminous.

The words tumble out of me, and dance like stars.

I have no idea how any of this has happened, just that it could not have happened any other way.

Afterwards they cheer. And then, one by one, come to cry in my arms—forming a line, dozens and dozens of them, each a hairy tangle of tears. These rough men, many of whom have committed the most heinous of crimes, some even court-ordered to be here, pried out of their straight world and dumped into this cauldron.

They don't know what to make of me, yet somehow have listened. Have seen past my faggotry, heard past my feminine voice, ignored all the cocks I have sucked.

They reach for me, begging for more. They don't even know what they want, just that they must have it, won't rest until they can get back to the incantation. That moment of mercy, when we were one.

I'm desperate to help them, and yet I'm spent, once again am nothing but me.

Eventually they give up, filing out of the room, on to their next session, not daring to linger any longer.

But what I remember most is their eyes, blazing with lightning that must yet land. And hours later at dinner, overhearing their amazement, as they brag to my partner.

His face crumpled, head shaking in confusion, that this must all be some mistake.

Most days we remain unseen. We just don't have the capacity to peer into each other's souls and hold our true potential. I won't see all of you, and you won't see all of me. And that just has to be okay. It simply means that it's incumbent upon each of us to shine. Not necessarily to take the room, but to permeate it with our radiance, to attract those that feel inspired. This is the essence of service work: less to impose our will on the world, than to embody our spiritual essence such that we might manifest our greatest good.

There is a paradox at play here: we are all in this together, but nobody can do it for us. Our personal growth and development journey starts with our individual efforts, our transformation. We may join with others in benevolent witness, but this work is ours alone. Even when we collaborate, we bring our personal work to the table. There it becomes the foundation for shared experience, learning, and growth. Our personal work is the soil in which the roots of the community tree are planted, fostered, and fixed. If we cease the work, the tree will wither and wane.

GETTING REAL ABOUT LIVING IN COMMUNITY

Our first work is with, for, and by ourselves. But what is it all for, unless we can then be of service to others? What good is a spirituality exclusively practiced in isolation? We are social creatures by nature. It is our human design. What a desolation to attempt this alone.

If anyone could have been an island, it would have been me. And I tried, oh how I tried. I shut myself off from the world and hid in my bunker. And yet there I was. And as invariably small as I made my life, there was still a spark: a tiny spark of loneliness, and a longing for others. Just when I thought I had outrun it, I would turn a corner only to face it again, confronted with the reality that I must live life on life's terms, which means in community.

To live in community means to live in service. One does not exist without the other. Some of us first learn this when we experience being part of a family, which requires us to subjugate our moods and whims. Some of us practice our service as part of a team, requiring us to hold the greater good above our own needs, whether in sports, music, theater, school, church, etc. The paradox is that through this teamwork, we cultivate enough sense of self and togetherness that we long to altruistically extend ourselves in service.

Don't get me wrong, we should not wait to be of service. There is no magic moment when we will one day have it all together. But we are wise to move slowly while we find our footing, lest we give more than we can afford at the risk of our recovery. I have often let my eagerness get the better of me, made unrealistic promises and commitments at the expense of sustaining my self-care. I've rushed in with blind enthusiasm, repeated old patterns like a fool in the fetter, only to have to apologize later and change course.

GETTING REAL ABOUT TAKING OWNERSHIP OF OUR LIVES

Life is not about eliminating our mistakes, but about reaching out with joy, and then cleaning up our messes. That is the essence of ownership. Not the ownership we take of items, but the ownership we take of our lives. Ownership is the natural consequence of empowerment. Taking ownership and becoming accountable is another way of standing tall in the world, a way of claiming our space, of being authentic and real.

We can demonstrate ownership in all facets of our lives: relationships with our loved ones, professional relationships, and anybody in our community. The moment we attempt to pass the buck, we hand over our power. The most effective way we can demonstrate ownership for our actions is by learning how to apologize effectively. We each make hundreds of mistakes a day. But how often do we take the time to own up to them, learn from them, and grow?

Here's what to do when making an apology:

- **Express your sorrow:** "I'm sorry for..."
- **Own your guilt:** "I was wrong when I..."
- **Name your specific wrongs:** "I did x, y, and z..."
- **Articulate the impact of your actions:** "I know that I hurt you when I...and it sounds like the consequences were..."
- **Make amends:** "What can I do to make this right?" (and then do it), or "Here's what I've done to make this right..."

Here's what NOT to do when making an apology:

- **Don't use "if statements":** "Sorry if I..."
- **Don't try to shift the blame or defend yourself:** "I know I did x, y, and z, but you..."
- **Don't use the passive voice:** "I'm sorry you were offended when..."

This process can seem time-consuming, cumbersome, and

uncomfortable at first. But it's a skill, not a talent. It can be learned, honed, and improved. And even more importantly, the results will speak for themselves. When you take the time to thoroughly and vulnerably own your actions, you will garner more trust from your loved ones, coworkers, and most everyone in your social orbit.

Ownership is an act of service. You will be most efficient and effective in your service of others when you are in command of your life. There are many forces that shape our lives, most of which are completely outside our control. Taking command of your life is less about determining outcomes, than understanding your place in the world, and shining with all your might; knowing where you both end and begin, and having the courage to unapologetically embody that entire space.

GETTING REAL ABOUT YOUR MISSION

Taking ownership of your life and getting empowered is essential to determining your mission. So many of us get hung up on life's larger questions, trying to determine what we are meant to do and why we're on this planet. While pondering the mysteries of the universe is an honorable pursuit, when it comes to your personal growth and development, I encourage you to be more pragmatic. Cultivating a mission is no different. We all have many twists and turns in our lives. You don't have to discern a single mission as an umbrella for all of your experiences. Instead, focus on choosing a mission for this moment.

What are you willing to commit to today? What about over the next few days and weeks? If you struggle to identify something, try keeping a daily journal, and look for the themes. In the various seasons of my life, I have committed to my marriage, my career, my passions, my health and wellness, service work, and all sorts of other aspirations. I have had such a varied career and wide range of experiences that I thought I might never find a through-line.

But over the course of several years, and with the help of both my life coach and my therapist, I began to notice some common themes. I finally crafted a mission statement that makes sense for me: *to serve others through art, advocacy, and strategic problem-solving.* This statement still holds true for me today, aligning my actions with my core beliefs. When I must make major life decisions, my mission statement gives me a sanity check. I expect this statement to serve me for a season, not a lifetime; once it no longer proves valuable, I will change it.

At this stage of your recovery, it's paramount you focus on a greater good. We can only keep what we give. If your mission is inwardly directed, it will not sustain you. For instance, if I create a mission to accumulate a million dollars just so it can sit untouched in my bank account, my prudent reserve might be flush, but my soul might feel unfed. Conversely, if I create a mission to accumulate a million dollars so I might fund philanthropic activities, then not only is my bank account happy, but my soul is nourished through the experience of joy and selflessness. My mind is stimulated by the work of managing the associated donations, and my heart is filled with the gratitude and comradery expressed during the donation process. When missions are larger than our own egos and fears, they feed us on multiple levels. And as we reap those rewards, we are encouraged to redouble our efforts, and build even more momentum.

GETTING REAL ABOUT YOUR VISION

Your vision is a view of your little slice of the world, as you think it could be—not as it *should* be. It can all sound so grandiose, but actually be quite simple. You get to choose your level of ambition. Perhaps your vision is living in a world free from poverty-induced hunger, or maybe it's something more easily attainable, such as living in a neighborhood without quite so much litter. Both are equally honorable.

Like your mission, your vision need not be an expression that lasts a lifetime. For many of us, that just feels like too large a chunk out of the apple. I've even written vision statements about specific events, situations, or periods of time. Here is a vision statement I wrote one year, as I prepared to welcome the spring season:

> To embody the spirit of spring and renewal, as well as the feeling of joy. To reconnect with current friends, and foster new ones. To cultivate a lighter touch and sense of play. To take risks and manifest a spirit of adventure.

I never learned how to play. I struggle with spontaneity and lightheartedness, yet both of these qualities are essential to serving my mission. In working with my life coach, I decided to draft this vision statement as a way to home in on these particular qualities. Some of you might have different approaches, or need to focus on different areas in your life. That's all okay.

I then used my vision statement as the basis for exploring

various supporting exercises. In one case, I wrote a meditation I could read daily to shape my experiences during the spring season:

> During this season, I envision a strong track record of success in manifesting the spirit of play, as well as a sense of vitality with current friends, new friends, and acquaintances in a variety of venues. Whether it's joking around with colleagues over the phone during work meetings, posting playful comments on Facebook, attending live sporting and arts events with my husband, attending and hosting dinner parties, or going to planned social events of all sorts, I will bring a spirit of joy and play. I will embody the season of spring and renewal, and bring a light touch to all I do. I will maintain regular contact with my inner child throughout the day. But most of all, I will embody the feeling of joy.

I was amazed at how putting pen to paper and articulating a clear, achievable vision shaped the contours of my experiences that spring. Writing my vision was another way of making a commitment. And once I had made that commitment, I found all sorts of supporting activities to ensure my success. That same spring I agreed to attend an intimidating social event, so I expanded the visioning exercise into a full-fledged meditation of how I wanted that evening to go.

My husband and I were scheduled to attend a fundraiser for a local queer performance artist. I'm reclusive, shy, and introverted; this is the very type of activity that still gives me anxiety. This artist is someone we have known for years. She is incredibly warm, kind, and gentle. She always does everything she can to greet us warmly and make us feel part of the group. Yet at previous fundraising events, thanks to various issues stemming from my core woundedness, I have still tended to melt into the background and hide behind my husband.

He is an extrovert, and much more adept than me at working a room. I know how to clown around, but often when I spend time in these types of social situations, it feels inauthentic: almost like some sort of performance art. I tend to leave the experience feeling physically drained and emotionally empty, even if others were amused and entertained by my "performance." In the past, it has just never seemed worth it.

That year, I was ready to do something different. I was ready to manifest power, presence, and purpose. So I created this vision I could use in my daily meditation:

> My husband and I arrive at the venue intentionally late. We are dressed in our most playful semi-formal attire. I'm wearing my favorite glittery tennis shoes, my nicest jeans, a tuxedo jacket, and a fun, hot pink t-shirt. I feel confident, at ease, and great about myself. I've been mentally preparing for this event for weeks, with visualizations and conversations with both my coach and my therapist. I've been working for months on building my confidence and self-esteem in all situations, and this party is an opportunity for socializing and fun. In fact, by the time the actual event rolls around I'm so confident that I'm actually looking forward to the chance to shine!

> When we arrive, our artist friend sees us right away and comes over to greet us. It's wonderful to see her, since we genuinely adore each other. She loves spending time with us, since we always make her laugh and make her feel so good about her art.

We chat for easily ten minutes, before she gets pulled away for more socializing. My husband and I look around the room for anyone else we might know. No such luck. Even though we're surrounded by new people, I feel completely at ease, since I know it will give me the chance to demonstrate all my progress and make some new connections.

My husband and I grab some wine and make our way to where a group of the artist's staff and collaborators are gathered. We introduce ourselves. Though they have met us before, they don't remember us. That's okay. We remind them that it's been a long time since we've seen them. Because we're so confident, it's easy for us to be gracious and emotionally available. We ask them about working with the artist, upcoming projects for their company, other artistic endeavors, inspiration, and all sorts of things. They love that we take such an interest in their work and radiate such warmth and kindness.

My husband heads off to grab some hors-d'oeuvres. I linger behind. I find myself making eye contact with another guest and ask how he knows the artist. We chat for a few minutes, and I learn about some of his hobbies and interests. Everything unfolds naturally, since I feel so confident, at-ease, and in alignment. He clearly enjoys our conversation, and I can feel the positive energy between us.

At some point, the conversation naturally concludes, and we move away from each other, deeper into the crowd. I feel happy about our conversation and excited at the prospect of meeting other new people. I look over and see my husband chatting with a group of women. Instead of rushing to his side, I continue to mingle. This makes me feel really good about myself: safe, secure, and strong.

I walk up to a small group of guys and introduce myself. I'm not nervous, because I know exactly who I am and why I'm here. In fact, I'm actually excited to get to know them. Not for any particular reason; they just look like nice guys. We make small talk, which I actually don't mind, since I know this is often how new friendships are born. It turns out they're actually really interesting, and they clearly think the same about me, since they keep asking me questions.

I'm so engrossed in the conversation, I don't even notice my husband come up behind me, until he puts his hand on my back, rubs it slightly, then slides his arms around my waist. I look over at him and smile, and then continue my conversation with the other guys. My husband lingers for a few moments, and then drifts away. This makes me feel so connected to him, but still safe and strong in my individuality.

Later the artist puts on a brief performance, before the official fundraising portion of the evening begins. We love watching her perform and laugh our butts off. After she performs, everybody applauds. My husband hoots and hollers. I laugh at him. I'm not embarrassed by him. I actually admire how playful and present he is. The artist's manager leads the fundraising event, and my husband and I contribute at the level we agreed upon and feel so happy to support her.

Afterwards, the artist thanks everyone. She picks us out of the crowd and heads over to us to give us a huge hug. We exchange some kind, heartfelt words before she heads off to socialize with others. She is clearly thrilled we came and makes sure we promise to say hello at her next performance. My husband and I leave the party, feeling happy, relaxed, and sated.

Adding this exercise to my daily meditation transformed my experience that year. I was able to attend the event and be my full, unapologetically weird self. I brought all of me, where in previous years I would have hidden away or left aspects of my personality at home. And when I look at photography from that event, I marvel at how safe I must have felt to appear so expressive. No more slinking in the shadows or playing it small. No more hiding in the bunker. No more locking myself away from the wonders of the world.

GETTING REAL ABOUT YOUR VALUES

I've yet to meet anybody who, at least in their heart of hearts, does not value service work. It's just part of our human design. Sure some might lack the capacity to serve in a specific way, but that does not negate the inner spark of joy we all feel whenever we can be of use. Some might act surly or grumpy about extending themselves in service, because they think they've been taken advantage of in the past. But I believe deep down even they want to lend a hand, because humans are wired that way. We just can't help it.

Itemizing your values is critical to understanding yourself on a deeper level. If you don't know what you hold dear, where will you seek refuge? What principles will drive your decisions, particularly when times are stressful? How will you know where to apply your efforts, even at a high level? What qualities will you see in others (friends, romantic partners, coworkers, etc.)?

Here are some of my values:

- Kindness
- Passion
- Compassion
- Love
- Integrity
- Wisdom
- Service
- Philanthropy
- Health
- Wellness
- Experience
- Humor
- Reliability
- Perseverance
- Dedication
- Determination
- Respect
- Generosity
- Peace
- Joy
- Intuition
- Intelligence

Our values inform our behavior. They are not just theoretical. They actually mean something practical, at least to the extent that we embody them.

There are several ways I keep these values front and center each day, in all that I do:

- **Meditation:** every morning I reflect on how I will embody, exude, and share my values with the world.
- **Physical Fitness:** each day I combine yoga, weightlift-

ing, and walking to create a balanced approach to taking care of my body.

- **Journaling:** every evening I reflect on my successes and failures as I seek to embody, exude, and share my values with the world.
- **Career:** I commit to balancing my values in all of my work, while taking the time to mentor and collaborate with others.
- **Marriage:** I use my passion to drive us forward (vision, dreams, goals, planning, etc.) and my kindness to temper the timelines, soften the approach, and ensure the sweetness of our connection (physical and emotional intimacy).
- **Friendships:** I leverage my passion to build friendships based on shared interests, and my kindness to nurture, grow, and deepen those friendships over time.

When you build a balanced life based on your values, you will invariably find yourself seeking to serve others, to share your rewards with the world. But we can only share what we have. It is critical we stay grounded in the daily practice of feeding ourselves first, so that we might break bread with others and use our gifts for the betterment of everyone.

GETTING REAL ABOUT YOUR OPPORTUNITIES TO SERVE

As you refine your practice and cultivate a space for service work, it's time to experiment with your efforts. This is the fun part! You get to try all sorts of avenues as you explore what fits your time and talents. Seek opportunities that fill your cup, while also improving the state of the world, or at least your little piece of it. There is no need to find causes that cost more than you can afford, whether in time, money, energy, or anything else. You won't earn extra points for martyrdom.

The point of self-sacrifice is not to endure undue deprivation or hardship, but to experience the momentary abnegation of self, as we enter the collective good. When we work, our self falls away and we enter a state of flow, where we are all one. It is unhealthy and impossible to attempt to permanently inhabit this realm of unity. We are designed to dip in and out of it, balancing self with oneness, and tempering togetherness with differentiation. In the same way, there are no enlightened people, only enlightened actions.

As you source opportunities for service work, be mindful of your capacity: logistically, physically, intellectually, and energetically. Here are some further guidelines to help ensure you only give what you can afford:

- **Availability:** How many hours each day or week can you afford to give to your service work? Is your schedule flexible? How will you balance this new commitment with existing ones?
- **Requirements:** What type of opportunities are you seeking (in other words, what are your requirements?) and what qualities are they seeking in their volunteers, staff, and assistants? Do you need any additional education, certifications, or credentials in order to qualify for open positions or opportunities? If so, do you currently have the capacity to earn these?
- **Morals:** Does the mission of the organization that you would like to serve align with your morals? If so, this work might yield multiple benefits. In addition to

enhancing the community, it might also embody and bring you in alignment with your own mission. If the organization's mission does not align with your morals, you will likely experience conflict at some point in your service. Think twice about this opportunity, since your time and energy might be better spent elsewhere.

- **Ethics:** How do the organization's mission, vision, and values align with standard best practices and industry mores? Are the leaders of this organization held in high esteem by the community and their peers? Or have they had challenges they have had to address? If so, how and when have they addressed them? Ensuring you save your energy for organizations that align with others in their category will set you up for long term success.

- **Culture:** How well do you like the other people in the organization? Do you feel like you can be all of yourself and still fit into the team? Or do they require you to shrink and self-censor? Remember, all things being equal, culture always wins. As a volunteer, it's unlikely you're going to be able to change an organization's culture, so if it's not a natural fit, it's probably best to apply your efforts elsewhere.

- **Unintended Consequences:** As a sanity check, what might be some of the potential unforeseen impacts of your work with this organization? Are you unintentionally overcommitting, which might thereby force you to reduce your efforts elsewhere? Are there any personal or professional risks for aligning with this organization? How will your work impact your body, mind, and spirit? Might the impact you make on this organization inadvertently and negatively impact other organizations or causes you hold dear?

I like to start with the easiest decisions first. For instance, why even address moral concerns if the service opportunity is outside the hours in which you are available? Or it requires more of a time commitment than you can afford? Combining criteria like this with your own self-study and meditation, as well as the counsel of your loved ones and trusted advisers, will help you make healthy and mutually beneficial decisions regarding where best to put your time and energy for service work.

GETTING REAL ABOUT THE REWARDS OF SERVICE WORK

Service work is not a one-way street. It need not be heroic or based in self-sacrifice. Not all service work need be performed for free. Volunteering is laudable, and it's also equally laudable to be well-compensated for sharing your gifts with the world. There is no shame in doing what you love, while helping your community, and earning enough money to pay your bills. It's honorable to reap the rewards of our work. In fact, it closes a loop: inspiration >> determination >> dedication >> perspiration >> compensation >> adulation. One leads to the other; rinse and repeat. There's simply no reason to shy away from the fruits of our labor.

Here are some of the rewards you might earn through your service work:

- **Professional Experience:** Not only are many types of future potential employers impressed with candidates who demonstrate a commitment to community engagement and improvement, but in some cases, you can develop direct or indirect subject matter expertise as part of your experience. This experience can even prove so valuable that you are able to explicitly add it to your portfolio or résumé.

- **Personal Experience:** Not all experience needs to be tied to subject matter expertise to prove valuable. Sometimes service work gives us the chance to learn or practice those soft skills that many prize, both in our personal and professional lives. But even more importantly, these personal experiences can enrich our lives, add meaning, and create purpose.

- **Professional Relationships:** In many cases, you will create new relationships with potential business and professional contacts solely by virtue of the fact that you engaged in service work. Chances are, you're not the only career-minded professional out there looking to round out their résumé. And even if you don't meet people directly in your industry or job function, your service work peers likely have contacts with others who work in your industry or job function. And of course, there's always the administrative staff of the organization that oversees your service work. Any number of these people will likely be so impressed with your efforts that they would be thrilled to write a letter of recommendation for you, serve as a reference, or help somewhere along the way.

- **Personal Relationships:** One of the best pieces of advice I could give anybody looking to make new friends or find romantic partners is to spend time serving your community in a way that you are passionate about. Not only will you impress others with your dedication and commitment, but you will be engaged in something you truly love—both of which are highly attractive to everyone! But more importantly, you will experience the joy of working side-by-side with others, engaged in a common cause. There's just nothing like being part of a team, and you will likely cherish these relationships for a lifetime.

Because there are so many ways we can potentially derive value from any opportunity, it's important to be mindful of our wants and needs. We are our own best advocates. It will feel much more empowering for us to explicitly present a case and make a request, than to sit back and cross our fingers. What are we hoping to gain from this experience? Why? How will we savor or utilize these rewards?

Perhaps we're not looking for any specific rewards, other than the satisfaction of our service, and that's okay too. Not all experiences need to be a means to an end. Sometimes the process is the whole point—pushing past our comfort zones and trying something new, simply for the sake of feeling more alive and connected with our community. If we cannot enjoy the doing of things, our life will seem like a crucible.

SUMMARY

Sometimes it can seem like the cards are so stacked against us as gay men that the best we can hope for is just to make it through another day. We only have just enough energy to wade through the bigotry of the straight world, earn some money, pay some bills, and hopefully have just a little bit of fun along the way—all without getting beat up or beat down. And if we're really lucky, maybe we scrape enough cash to sock a little away for a rainy day. Maybe meet someone nice who's into us and we ignite a mutual spark.

I believe this vision is not enough. We all have the capacity to one day take the world by storm. We have it in us to make waves. But for this to happen, most of us need a plan. We need a clear sense of our mission, vision, and values, such that we can embolden and embody our spirit, and then push that into the world through service. While we are working on our big plans, we all have the capacity to do something utterly decadent and soul-feeding to sustain us now. So today I encourage you to do at least one sweet thing, just for yourself, and then abide in the wisdom of that singular joy.

Were there an ending to our personal growth and development, service work would be the capstone. But the reality is that we are forever works in progress: changing, evolving, growing, deepening, learning, failing, succeeding, synthesizing, and integrating. There is no finish line, and no reason to wait for any particular milestone or time frame to begin the practice of service work. What's important is that we identify our assets and liabilities, understand our strengths and weaknesses, earn our limits, and harness all that we know, so we can immediately start improving our lives and the world. Right here. Right now. Today. Because that's the meaning of life: to share our light, our love, and all that has been given to us.

We are proud gay men: complex mixtures of privilege and adversity, beloved members of the rich LGBTQIA+ community, and essential to the panoply of our pluralistic society. We own all that we are and shrink from no one. Our culture is real and has value; we refuse to be subsumed into the mainstream. We are nobody's caricature or life accessory, nobody's punching bag or doormat. When called to arms, we fight. But we also tend the wounded; we nurture and support those that let us. We are fathers and brothers and sons. We are friends and coworkers and lovers. We laugh, we love, we live, we breathe. Vibrantly. Together. So come warm your hands by the gentle fire of life, and let your heart be healed. Then let's go out there and make an impact. Get real, stand tall, and take your place. No excuses, and no regrets. Just grab the apple, take a big bite, and savor it all!

ACKNOWLEDGMENTS

First, I want to thank my husband, Scott. He not only has lived with all the ups and downs of the writing process, but has stood with me for the past decade. That has included graduate school, job changes, vision quests, and all my other grand experiments. Scott also took the time to read each chapter of this book before I released it to the world. He helped keep me grounded, centered, and in touch with my deepest truths. All my love.

I also want to thank my coach, Jonathan Beal. Hiring him has been one of the best decisions I have ever made. In fact, writing this book was his idea! Without Jonathan's confidence in me, my journey, and my ability to positively contribute to the lives of gay men, I never would have considered writing a book like this. He has coached me in my career, my health and fitness, as well as my personal growth and development. You can learn more about Jonathan's work here: jonathangarybeal.com

I want to thank Dan Buchanan, my longtime therapist, for teaching me how to love myself, for holding my story and believing in me because of it, and for seeing the best in me, even amidst my fears and self-doubt. He is a continual source of inspiration. You can learn more about Dan's work here: olympiccounseling.com

I would also like to thank Zach Bulls and Andrew Sartory, as well as the entire team at Gay Man Thriving: Audrey, Drew, Craig, Terry, and Nick. They were all so supportive and amazing over the course of this journey, while also allowing me to assist in their mission to empower gay men to find the relationships of their dreams. The community they have built is responsible for so much light and love in the lives of gay men around the world, and I could not be prouder to have been along for the ride! You can learn more about this wonderful movement here: gaymanthriving.com

I want to thank Steve Granville, my small group teacher during my time at the Hoffman Institute. Even though our time together was brief, his impact on my life was profound. During my Hoffman journey, he was a both a beacon and a bulwark. He immediately opened his heart to me with words of safety and encouragement. But what I will never forget is the lightness and depth of his spirit, calling forth my own to be a better person, and then showing me the way. You can read more about the Hoffman Process here: hoffmaninstitute.org

I am so grateful for my editor, Suzanne Lahna. Their meticulous attention to detail, profound sense of professionalism, and relentless drive for inclusivity ensured this material would be presented in its best light. It was so important to me to work with an editor from the LGBTQIA+ community on this project, but I never dreamed I would be so fortunate to find someone as talented as Suzanne. You can learn more about their services here: the-quick-fox.com

To the entire publishing team at Scribe, thank you from the bottom of my heart: Emily Anderson, Hal Clifford, Erin Tyler, Rachel Brandenburg, Tiffany Fletcher, Josh Raymer, Zach Obront, and others. Each of you are amazing, and I could not have done any of this without you! You can learn more about their services here: scribewriting.com

Special thanks to Malcolm Powers for the cover photograph.

ABOUT THE AUTHOR

BRITT EAST is an author and speaker who uses his experience, strength, and hope to challenge and inspire change-oriented gay men to get down to the business of improving their lives. With over two decades of personal growth and development experience in a variety of modalities, such as the 12 Steps, Nonviolent Communication, yoga, meditation, talk therapy, and the Hoffman Process, Britt is committed to building a personal practice of self-discovery that he can then share with gay men everywhere. He lives in Seattle with his husband and their crazy dog. Learn more about him at britteast.com.

CPSIA information can be obtained
at www.ICGtesting.com
Printed in the USA
FSHW011418140221
78568FS